creating
a web site
with flash

Visual QuickProject Guide

by David Morris

Peachpit
Press

Visual QuickProject Guide
Creating a Web Site with Flash
David Morris

Peachpit Press

1249 Eighth Street
Berkeley, CA 94710
510/524-2178
800/283-9444
510/524-2221 (fax)

Find us on the Web at www.peachpit.com.
To report errors, please send a note to errata@peachpit.com.
Peachpit Press is a division of Pearson Education.

Editor: Rebecca Gulick
Production Editor: Hilal Sala
Compositor: Owen Wolfson
Indexer: FireCrystal Communications
Interior Design: Elizabeth Castro
Cover Design: The Visual Group with Aren Howell
Cover Production: Owen Wolfson
Cover Photo Credit: Photodisc

Notice of Rights

Notice of Liability

The information in this book is distributed on an "As Is" basis, without warranty. While every precaution has been taken in the preparation of the book, neither the author nor Peachpit Press shall have any liability to any person or entity with respect to any loss or damage caused or alleged to be caused directly or indirectly by the instructions contained in this book or by the computer software and hardware products described in it.

Trademarks

ISBN 0-321-32125-1

9 8 7 6 5 4 3

Printed and bound in the United States of America

For Duane,

My endless source of strength, hope, and love.

Special thanks to...

Liz Dobecka and Timeless Blooms, for graciously agreeing to be my design guinea pig. I hope I did justice to your beautiful works.

Leigh Rountree, for providing such a solid base of content for me to lift and mangle.

My editor, Rebecca Gulick, for the hand-holding and for making it all much better than it was.

Nancy Davis, for shepherding this great book series and for giving me this opportunity.

And finally, Marjorie Baer, who remembered me from another life and was such an enthusiastic advocate. Thanks so much. I owe you many dinners.

contents

contents

introduction

The Visual QuickProject Guide that you hold in your hands offers a unique way to learn about new technologies. Instead of drowning you in theoretical possibilities and lengthy explanations, this Visual QuickProject Guide uses big, color illustrations coupled with clear, concise step-by-step instructions to show you how to complete one specific project in a matter of hours.

Our project in this book is to create a beautiful, engaging Web site using Macromedia Flash. Our Web site showcases a small, home-based business, but since the project covers all the basic techniques, you'll be able to use what you learn to create your own Flash-based Web sites—perhaps to promote your own business, showcase a hobby or collection, or provide a site for your neighborhood association.

what you'll create

This is the home page of the Timeless Blooms Web site, the project you'll create. In the process, you'll learn the following useful techniques:

Create interactive buttons for navigation between the different sections of your site.

Draw graphic elements to define your site's look and feel.

Import graphics and images created in other applications.

Animate text to provide interest and a professional quality.

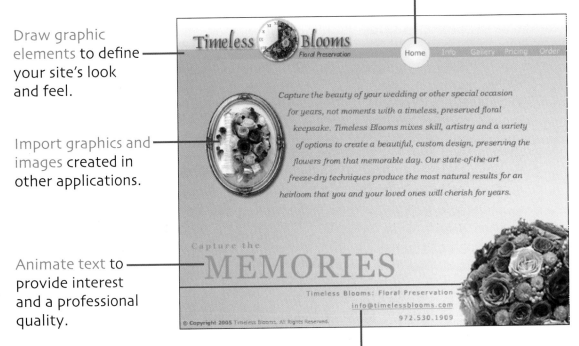

Format text in the font, size, and color of your choice.

Add progress bars to update viewers about download progress of large movies.

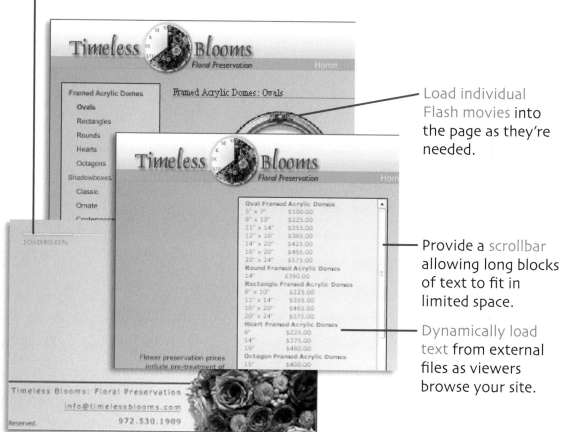

Load individual Flash movies into the page as they're needed.

Provide a scrollbar allowing long blocks of text to fit in limited space.

Dynamically load text from external files as viewers browse your site.

how this book works

The title of each section explains what is covered in that section.

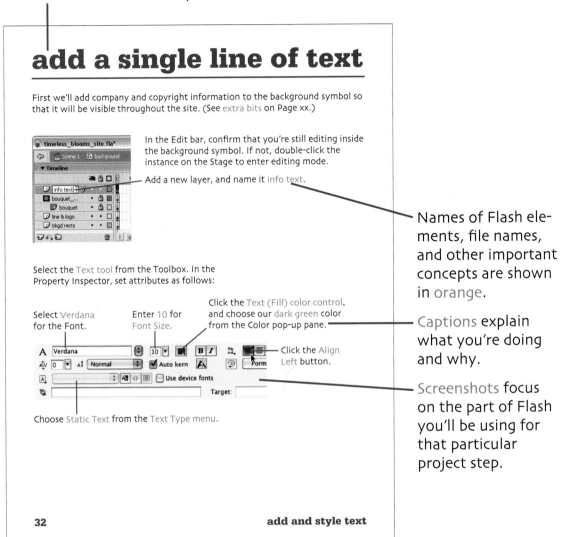

add a single line of text

First we'll add company and copyright information to the background symbol so that it will be visible throughout the site. (See extra bits on Page xx.)

In the Edit bar, confirm that you're still editing inside the background symbol. If not, double-click the instance on the Stage to enter editing mode.

Add a new layer, and name it info text.

Names of Flash elements, file names, and other important concepts are shown in orange.

Select the Text tool from the Toolbox. In the Property Inspector, set attributes as follows:

Select Verdana for the Font.

Enter 10 for Font Size.

Click the Text (Fill) color control, and choose our dark green color from the Color pop-up pane.

Click the Align Left button.

Captions explain what you're doing and why.

Screenshots focus on the part of Flash you'll be using for that particular project step.

Choose Static Text from the Text Type menu.

add and style text

introduction

The extra bits section at the end of each chapter contains additional tips and tricks that you might like to know but that aren't absolutely necessary for creating the Web page.

extra bits

draw background elements p. 11

- In Flash, when an object is overlapping another, the overlapped section of the existing object is deleted. This makes adjustments such as nudging new objects into place a nightmare. To avoid this, you can either create a new layer for every object you draw or group an object as soon as you draw it. I prefer grouping.

create reusable graphics p. 18

- Using symbols in Flash provides two main benefits: reduced file size and ease of editing.
- When you create a symbol and place instances of that symbol on the Stage, your movie's file size is reduced because no matter how many times you use it, the code required to define it is only included in the file once. Each instance just points to the symbol and describes any modifications to that symbol, such as transparency or size.
- Modifying work later is also much easier. Imagine that you've placed 100 blue squares (not instances of a blue square symbol) throughout your movie, and then you decide

to change the color. You have to find and change all 100 squares. But if you made a symbol of a blue square and placed 100 instances, you only have to change the symbol, and the 100 instances are updated automatically.

edit a symbol p. 19

- When you have an object on the Stage that is a container for other objects (groups, symbols and text boxes) you can just double-click it to "get inside" and edit the contents.
- To exit the editing mode of the container, you can double-click outside the bounds of the container.
- Sometimes when you draw a line in Flash, it isn't placed at the top of the object stacking order like you'd expect it to be. Instead, it is placed behind other objects. Defying the standard convention that a new object is stacked above existing objects on the same layer, Flash stacks lines based on a mysterious formula involving the line's color that only programmers could come up with!

The heading for each group of tips matches the section title. (The colors are just for decoration and have no hidden meaning.)

Next to the heading there's a page number that also shows which section the tips belong to.

design the layout of your stage   29

companion web site

You can find this book's companion site at http://www.peachpit.com/vqj/flash.

In the Support Files section of the site, you'll find all of the files you need to complete the project in this book. You can also download the intermediate files created in each chapter and the files that make up the final project site.

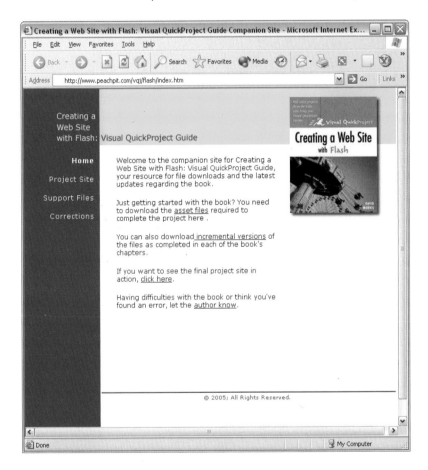

Visit the Project Site section to see a completed example of the site you're building in this book.

You can also find any updated material in the Corrections section of the site.

explore flash

At first glance the Flash interface can be overwhelming with its many panels and controls, but don't be concerned. As you progress through this project, you'll learn how to access the important stuff and how to harness all the power of Flash. When you finish the project, you'll have the knowledge and skills needed to create a professional-quality Web site to suit your business, organization, or personal needs.

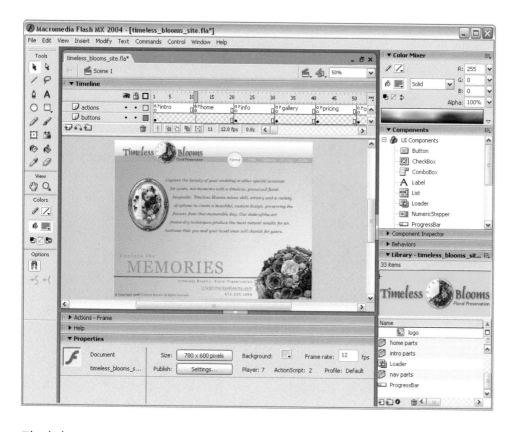

Flash borrows many of its conventions and terms from film production. The presentation you create for viewers is a movie, the distinct parts of the movie are scenes, the players (your content) are on the Stage, and movement through time is accomplished via the Timeline. Thinking about the Flash interface in the context of this film metaphor will help you quickly grasp the way we work in Flash. We are producing a movie that features your content and tells the story you want Web viewers to see. (See extra bits on Page xx.)

explore flash (cont.)

The story you're telling with your movie is presented on the Stage. You'll use it as your workspace to place and arrange the elements of your site. The Stage's rectangular dimensions define the area of your movie that viewers will see.

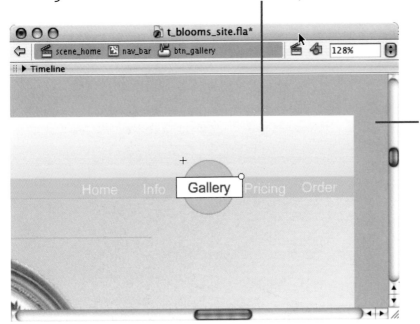

Gray space around the Stage makes up the Work Area, which holds objects that hang off the Stage and animated elements that move onto or off of the Stage. To view or hide objects in the Work Area, choose View > Work Area, or press Ctrl Shift w (Windows) or Cmd Shift w (Mac).

In Flash, you'll often find yourself drilled down multiple levels within elements, such as editing text that is inside a button symbol inside a movie placed in a particular scene. The Edit bar at the top of the window displays those levels to help keep you oriented and to let you quickly backtrack when your edit is complete. Additionally, you can use it to navigate between scenes, to locate and modify symbols, and to change view magnification.

The Tools panel is the toolbox you'll use to draw objects, create text, and modify the elements of your movie. The Tools panel also provides control to change your view of the Stage, modify colors, and set options for the tools you choose.

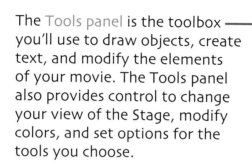

Review and change the attributes of objects in the Property Inspector. Controls in the Property Inspector change dynamically, displaying the attributes and settings relevant to your current selection. Here you'll be able to modify the attributes of text, graphics, frames, animations, and more.

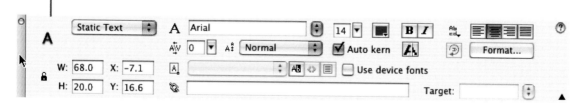

explore flash (cont.)

The Timeline controls the order, timing and flow of your movie. The panel contains three primary sections: frames, layers, and the Playhead.

The Playhead indicates the current frame displayed on the Stage.

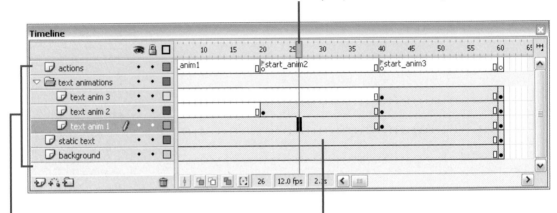

Think of layers as independent strips of film, each containing its own objects, stacked on top of one another, and composited to present a particular frame. In most cases, each layer we create will contain only a few objects, making it easier to keep track of things as the project gets progressively more complex.

Frames in the Timeline represent changes in your content over time. However it's important to think of frames as something more than just for animation; frames also serve an important function as milestones within your site to which you can link other content.

If the elements in your movie are the players, then symbols are the featured stars. Using symbols, which we'll learn more about later, decreases file size, saves time on edits, and organizes your file. The symbols in your movie are stored and accessed from the Library panel.

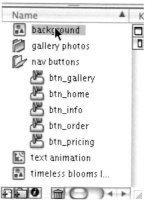

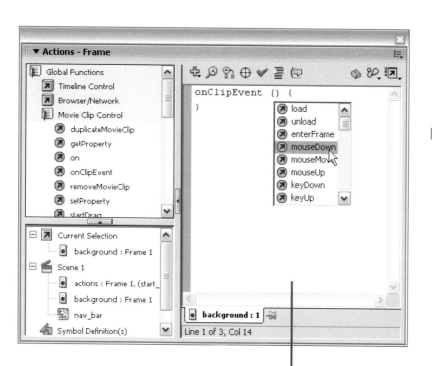

The Actions panel is used for adding ActionScript to your movie. ActionScript is Flash's scripting language for adding complex interactivity, controlling navigation, and programming many of the advanced functions found in robust Flash applications. As you can imagine, it can be a daunting task to script a movie, but don't worry. We'll use the simplified process provided in the Behaviors panel and have minimal use for the Actions panel in our project.

explore flash (cont.)

The Behaviors panel provides the power and control of ActionScript without your having to code the script yourself. Behaviors are prepackaged bits of ActionScript presented with interfaces that allow you to easily set up complex interactions that would otherwise require coding.

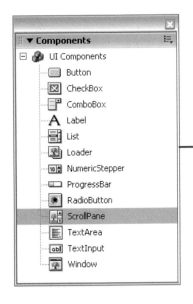

If Behaviors are packages of ActionScript that you apply to objects in your file, components, accessed from the Components panel, are packages of special-purpose objects that include the ActionScript to control their behavior. Components include simple user interface controls, such as buttons and checkboxes, and more complex controls that contain content such as scroll panes and windows.

After you add a component to your file, you'll use the Component Inspector to specify parameters specific to the component type and your particular design requirements.

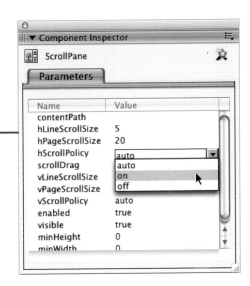

the next step

While this Visual QuickProject Guide teaches you the basics for creating a Web site in Flash, there is much more to learn. If you're curious about Flash development, try Macromedia Flash MX 2004 for Windows and Macintosh: Visual QuickStart Guide, by Katherine Ulrich. It features clear examples, simple step-by-step instructions, and loads of visual aids to cover every aspect of Flash design.

After that, you can take it to the next level with Macromedia Flash MX 2004 Advanced for Windows and Macintosh: Visual QuickPro Guide, by Russell Chun and Joe Garraffo.

extra bits

explore flash p.xiii

- Avoid the temptation to "store" unused objects offstage in the work area; they'll still be exported in the final movie and will add to the file size, prolonging download times.

- Clicking the small triangle-shaped icon in the bottom-right corner of the Property Inspector toggles visibility of the bottom half of the panel, which contains controls that are considered secondary. Hiding these controls is not recommended for the novice so that you don't wasted time hunting around the application when you do need them.

- The Library panel in Flash differs from other panels because you can have multiple instances of it open at the same time—one for each Flash document you have open. While handy, it can also be confusing when you want to access a symbol but are looking at another document's library. For easy identification, the name of the file is appended to the panel title.

- Need a custom user interface element that's not included in Flash installed components? Many custom components can be found on the Macromedia Exchange for you to download and install. The Exchange is located at: http://www.macromedia.com/exchange

1. prepare your site files

Before you begin the design and development of your Web site, it's important to get organized.

In this chapter, we set up a directory structure for all of our files, create and save the Flash file that will be our site movie, and define the color scheme that we'll use throughout the site.

If you haven't already done so, download the asset files for the Timeless Blooms Web site from this book's companion site at www.peachpit.com/vqj/flash.

define folder structure

Before beginning work on our Flash movie, you need to set up a hierarchy of folders and files on your computer's desktop. Within this structure we'll have two discreet folder sets: one for files that we'll use during the development of the site and one for files that will be uploaded to the Web.

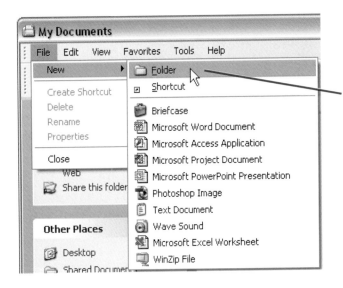

From the Windows Explorer or Mac OS's Finder, choose File > New > Folder to create the parent directory. Name the folder timeless_blooms_website.

Open the timeless_blooms_website folder, and create two new folders. Name one site_files and one development_files.

Copy the asset files that you downloaded from this book's companion site into the development_files folder.

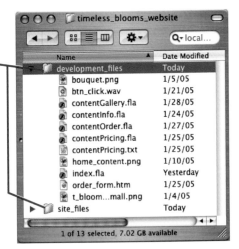

prepare your site files

create your site file

There are two types of Flash files that we'll be working with. A FLA file is the working file you create in Flash and do all of your design and development in. FLA files are opened only with Flash. At the other end of the process, a SWF file is the file you export from Flash and post on the Web. The SWF file is your Flash movie and can be opened by browsers, the Flash Player, and some other applications.

Launch Flash, and choose File > New to create your FLA file.

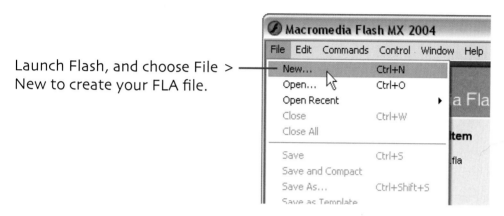

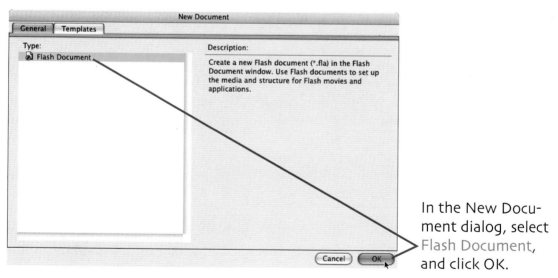

In the New Document dialog, select Flash Document, and click OK.

set canvas properties

Flash defaults to a canvas size of 550 x 400 pixels with a white background. Let's change those settings to fit the needs of our project.

If the Property Inspector is not visible, choose Window > Properties to open it.

In the Property Inspector, click the Document Properties button. This is a bit confusing, since the button is next to a label that reads Size and the text on the button shows the canvas dimensions. Even so, this is the Document Properties button.

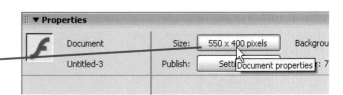

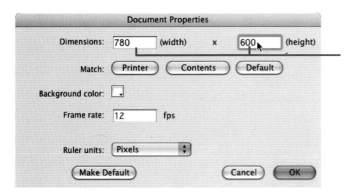

In the Document Properties dialog, enter 780 for the width and 600 for the height.

Next, click the Background Color control to open the Color pop-up pane.

In the Hex Edit text field, select the text #FFFFFF, replace it with #CBE6B2, and press ⎆Enter. Click OK to exit the Document Properties dialog.

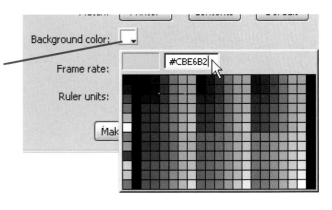

4

save your file

Before going any further, you should save your file. Choose File > Save, or press Ctrl S (Windows) or ⌘ S (Mac).

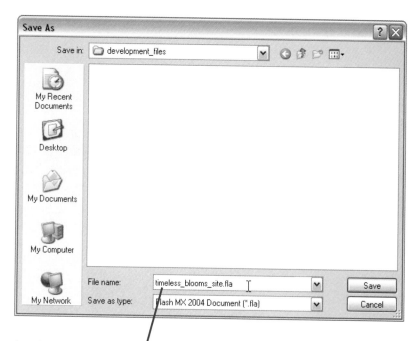

In the Save As dialog, navigate to the development_files folder we created earlier. Enter timeless_blooms_site.fla for the file name, and click Save.

I'll remind you to save your work at the end of each chapter, but you should keep in mind the old edict "Save early and often."

save your color scheme

To make applying our color scheme easier and to speed development, we'll first add the colors for our site to the Color Swatches panel, where they can be easily accessed from any of Flash's color pop-up windows. (See extra bits on Page 8.)

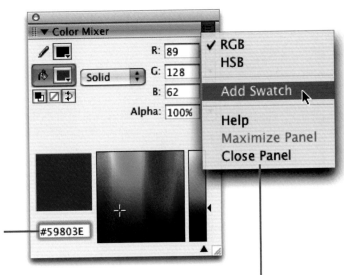

1 If it's not already visible, open the Color Mixer panel (Window > Design Panels > Color Mixer, or press (Shift)(9)). To define the dark green color, enter the hex color value #59803E in the Hex value field at the bottom left of the panel.

2 On the right of the panel's title bar, click the Options menu icon, and choose Add Swatch.

prepare your site files

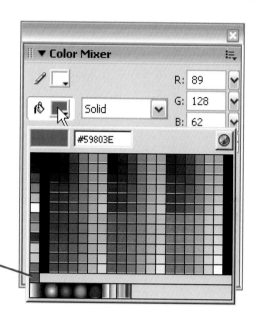

Click one of the color wells in the panel to open the swatches pop-up. Notice that our dark green color has been added to the bottom row of swatches.

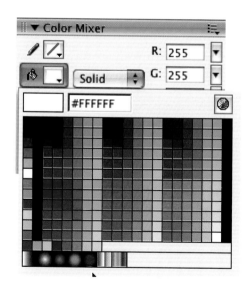

Repeat steps 1 and 2 to add the other colors to the swatches.

Medium Green: #99CC66

Light Green: #CBE6B2

Dark Rose: #94214F

Medium Rose: #CC2C66

Light Rose: #DA7EA1

Dark Yellow: #F1DC95

Light Yellow: #FFE89E

extra bits

save your color scheme p. 6

- Choosing the color scheme for your Web site is an important first step in the design phase of development. Here are a couple tips to keep in mind:

  Limit the number of colors used in your design. Too many colors make the design look chaotic and cluttered.

  Pick two or three main colors, and then use different tints of those colors for highlights, backgrounds, etc.

  If your organization has a color logo or a primary graphic for the home page, pull colors from that existing artwork, or choose colors that are complimentary.

prepare your site files

2. design the layout of your stage

Our first task in Web site development is to design the visual framework within which all of our content will be presented. Think of it as dressing the set of your movie: providing the backdrop, defining different regions, and making it visually attractive. Along the way we'll learn how to use many of Flash's most basic functions. The following are some of the tasks we'll cover:

Import and transform vector artwork.

Save reusable objects, called symbols, for easy modification and smaller movie file size.

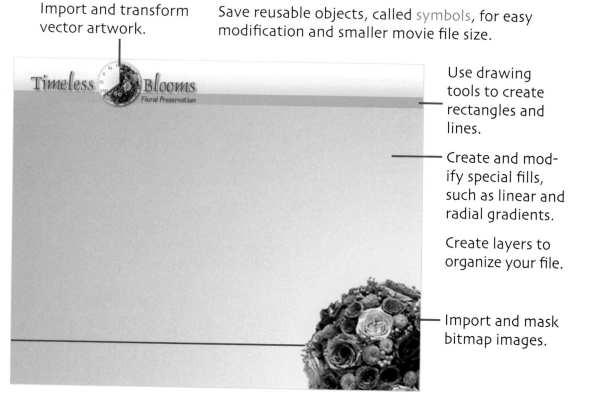

Use drawing tools to create rectangles and lines.

Create and modify special fills, such as linear and radial gradients.

Create layers to organize your file.

Import and mask bitmap images.

set up guides

Using guides in your file helps you define areas of your Stage and eases placement of objects. Let's add some guides before we begin drawing our background.

1 Choose Window > Design Panels > Info to launch the Info panel.

2 Choose View > Rulers to turn on rulers along the left and top of the Stage.

3 Click and drag down a guide from the horizontal (top) ruler. Watch the Info panel; when the cursor location's y value is 60, release the mouse. Drag out two more rules at 80 and 520.

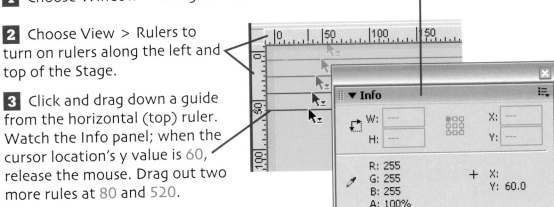

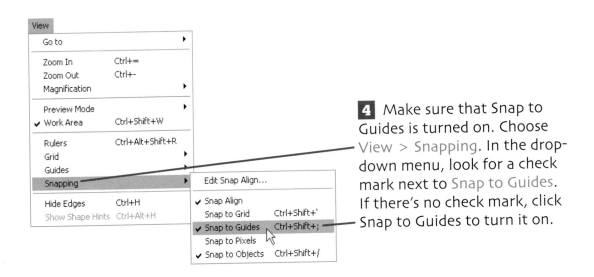

4 Make sure that Snap to Guides is turned on. Choose View > Snapping. In the drop-down menu, look for a check mark next to Snap to Guides. If there's no check mark, click Snap to Guides to turn it on.

design the layout of your stage

draw background

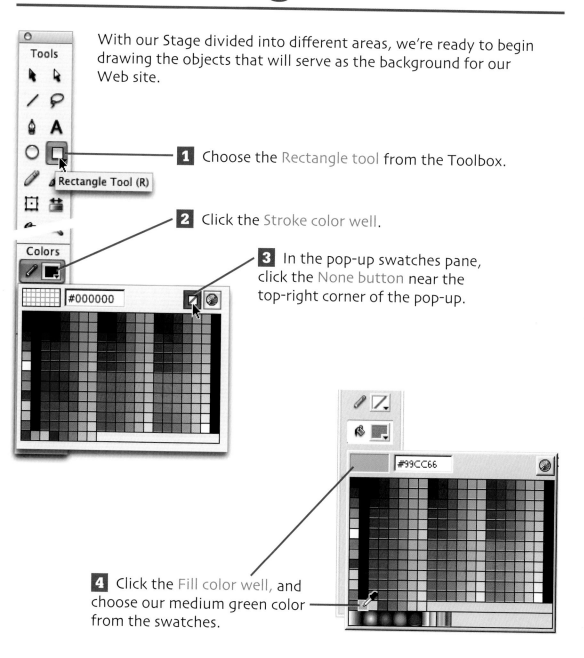

With our Stage divided into different areas, we're ready to begin drawing the objects that will serve as the background for our Web site.

1 Choose the Rectangle tool from the Toolbox.

Rectangle Tool (R)

2 Click the Stroke color well.

3 In the pop-up swatches pane, click the None button near the top-right corner of the pop-up.

#000000

#99CC66

4 Click the Fill color well, and choose our medium green color from the swatches.

draw background (cont.)

Position the cursor at the left edge of the Stage on top of the guide you placed at 60. Click and drag out a rectangle to the right edge of the Stage and down to the guide at 80.

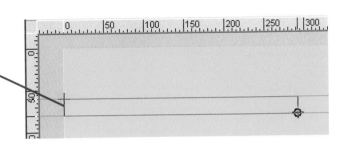

1 You can make adjustments to the rectangle if size or placement is a little off. Choose the Selection tool from the Toolbox, and click the rectangle to select it.

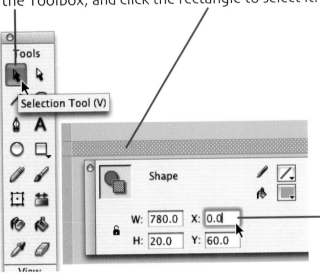

2 In the Property Inspector you can change the values in the width, height, x-position, and y-position text fields. Our rectangle should be 780 x 20 pixels and placed at 0 x-position and 60 y-position.

With the rectangle still selected, choose Modify > Group. (See extra bits on Page 29.)

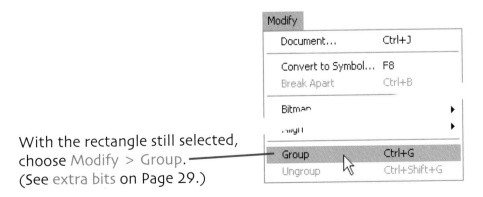

design the layout of your stage

add linear gradient

Next we'll draw some background rectangles with gradient fills to give our Stage some visual interest.

Choose the Rectangle tool. Set the Stroke color well to None, and the Fill color well to any color you choose—we'll change it in a moment.

Click and drag out a rectangle from the top-left corner of the Stage (0,0) to the top of the medium green rectangle and the right edge of the Stage.

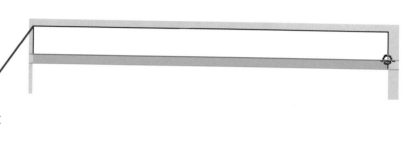

In the Color Mixer, click the Fill Style drop-down menu, and select Linear.

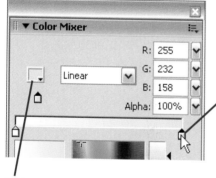

1 You'll see a new control on the panel—a gradient definition bar with pointers below the bar indicating each color in the gradient. Click the pointer on the right end of the gradient definition bar.

2 The color represented by the pointer will now appear in the Color Proxy color well next to the Fill Style menu.

add linear gradient (cont.)

3 Click the Color Proxy color well to open the swatches pop-up. Choose our light green color.

4 The pointer on the left of the gradient definition bar should already be set to white. If it's not, change it now.

5 Choose the Paint Bucket tool, and click on the solid-filled rectangle you drew earlier.

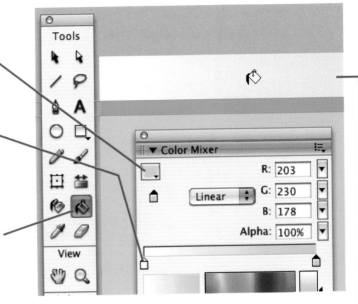

6 Now the rectangle has a white-to-green gradient fill. It's not in the direction we want, so we'll change that next.

design the layout of your stage

edit linear gradient

Choose the Fill Transform tool, and click the rectangle to select it.

Three editing handles appear:

a round handle to reposition the center point of the gradient

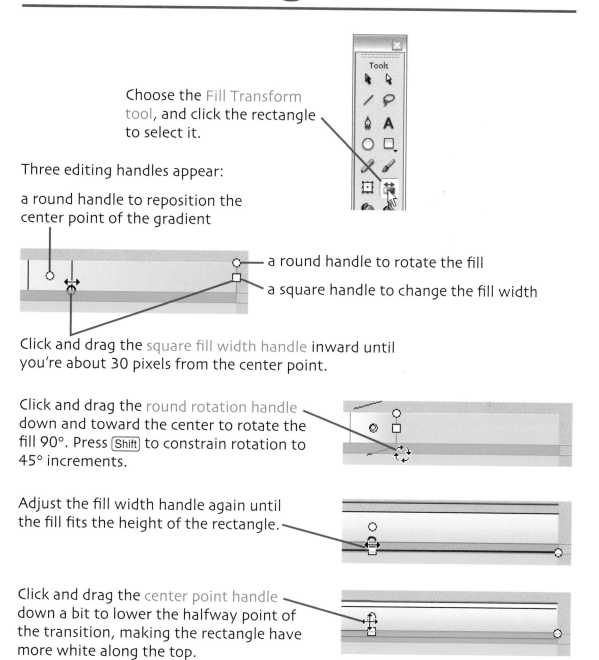

— a round handle to rotate the fill

— a square handle to change the fill width

Click and drag the square fill width handle inward until you're about 30 pixels from the center point.

Click and drag the round rotation handle down and toward the center to rotate the fill 90°. Press Shift to constrain rotation to 45° increments.

Adjust the fill width handle again until the fill fits the height of the rectangle.

Click and drag the center point handle down a bit to lower the halfway point of the transition, making the rectangle have more white along the top.

Select the rectangle with the Selection tool, and choose Modify > Group.

design the layout of your stage

create radial gradients

Now let's draw the final rectangle, which will make up our Stage's background.

Select the Rectangle tool.

Set the Stroke color well to None.

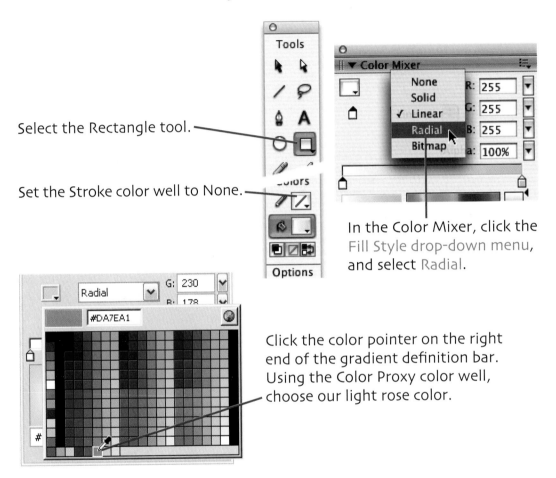

In the Color Mixer, click the Fill Style drop-down menu, and select Radial.

Click the color pointer on the right end of the gradient definition bar. Using the Color Proxy color well, choose our light rose color.

design the layout of your stage

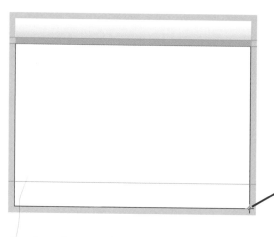

Now, move the cursor to the left edge of the Stage and the bottom of the solid green rectangle (0,80). Click and drag out a rectangle to the bottom-right corner of the Stage.

Again, the gradient is there, but it's not quite what we want. Let's change it.

In order to see a large part of the Work Area surrounding the Stage, choose View > Magnification > 25%.

Select the Fill Transform tool, and click the rectangle to select it. Four editing handles appear:

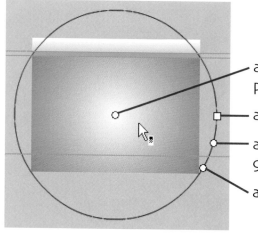

a round handle to reposition the center point of the gradient

a square handle to change the fill width

a round handle to change the radius of the gradient

a round handle to rotate the fill

design the layout of your stage

radial gradients (cont.)

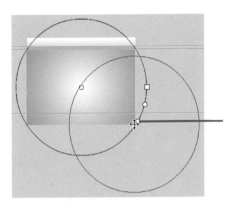

Click and drag the round center point handle to the bottom-right corner of the Stage.

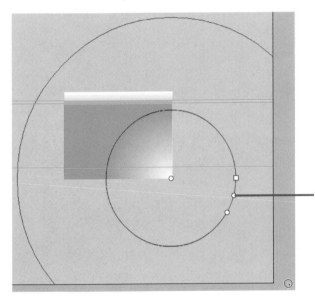

Click and drag the middle round handle, enlarging the circle beyond the top-left corner of the Stage.

Change the view back to the magnification you like to work at. Select the rectangle, and group it (Modify > Group).

reusable graphics

Since our background is the same throughout our Web site, we can reuse what we've drawn multiple times. To do that, we need to convert our three rectangles into one reusable symbol. When a symbol is used on the Stage, it's called an instance. (See extra bits on Page 29.)

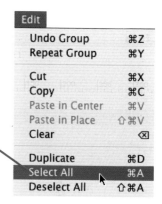

To select the three rectangles, choose Edit > Select All, or press ⌃A (Windows) or ⌘A (Mac).

Choose Modify > Convert to Symbol, or press F8.

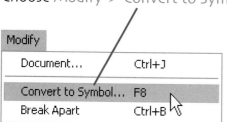

In the Convert to Symbol dialog, name the symbol background.

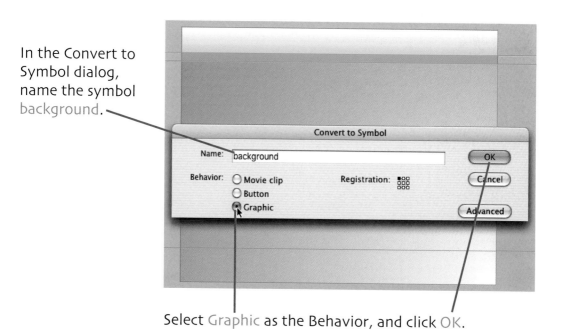

Select Graphic as the Behavior, and click OK.

reusable graphics (cont.)

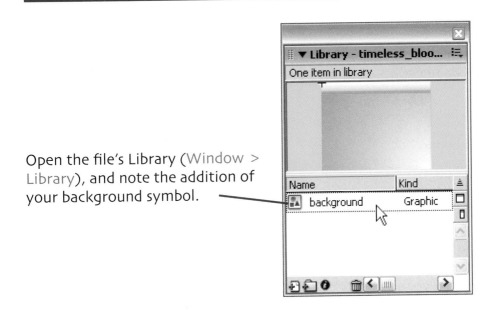

Open the file's Library (Window > Library), and note the addition of your background symbol.

You'll also notice in the Property Inspector that new controls have appeared, reflecting the selection of the symbol instance.

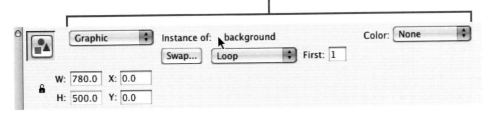

edit a symbol

Let's edit the symbol to add a line.
(See extra bits on Page 30.)

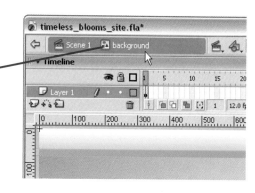

Double-click the symbol to enter symbol-
editing mode. The Info bar above the Stage
shows what container you're editing.

1 From the Toolbox, select the Line tool.

2 In the Property Inspector,
click the Stroke color well, and
choose our dark rose color.

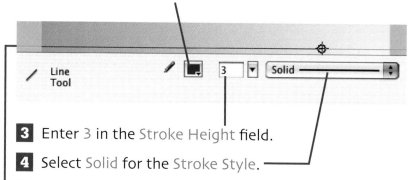

3 Enter 3 in the Stroke Height field.

4 Select Solid for the Stroke Style.

5 Click and drag out a line on the guide we placed at y-location 520 and drag
from the left edge of the Stage to the right edge.

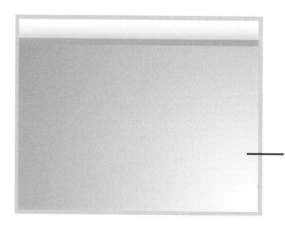

Press Ctrl ; (Windows) or ⌘ ; (Mac)
to turn off guides.

It appears that the line isn't there,
but it is; it's just underneath the rose-
gradient rectangle. We'll fix that in
the next section.

organize with layers

Layers, as we outlined before, are great organizational tools. They control the stacking order of objects in your movie. We're going to create a new layer above the current one and move our hidden line there.

First, let's rename the current layer to reflect what it contains.

If the Timeline isn't already visible, choose Window > Timeline. In the Layers column, double-click the text Layer 1 to select it. Enter bkgd rects for the layer name, and press ⏎Enter.

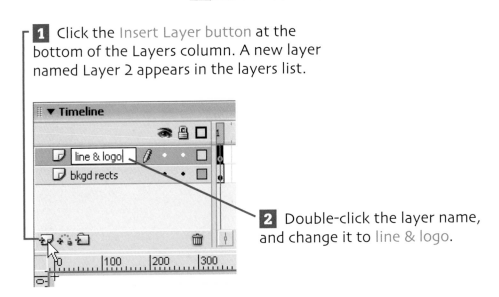

1 Click the Insert Layer button at the bottom of the Layers column. A new layer named Layer 2 appears in the layers list.

2 Double-click the layer name, and change it to line & logo.

design the layout of your stage

move between layers

Moving objects from one layer to another in Flash works differently than in most drawing applications. Here's how it's done.

With the Selection tool, click in the Work Area to the left of the Stage, and drag a selection marquee around the area where you know your line is. Turn on Show Guides (View > Guides > Show Guides) if you need a visual clue of the line's location.

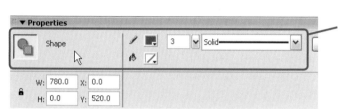

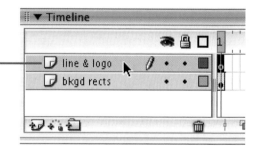

Although you still can't see the line, you'll know it's selected because of the feedback in the Property Inspector.

Choose Edit > Cut to move the line from the bkgd rects layer to the clipboard.

In the Timeline, click the line & logo layer to make it the active layer.

Choose Edit > Paste in Place to paste the line into the exact same location, just on the different layer.

Finally! We can see our line now. It was a lot of effort, but isn't it a beautiful line?

design the layout of your stage   **23**

import vector art

Sometimes you'll need to add artwork that has been created in another application or file format to your Flash movie. Here, we're going to import logo artwork that's been provided in a Macromedia Fireworks' PNG file that contains vectors (editable paths) and bitmap objects (images).

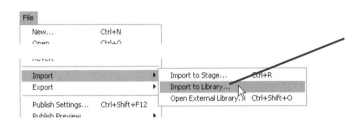

Choose File > Import > Import to Library to insert the logo file into your movie as a symbol.

In the Import to Library dialog, locate the file t_blooms logo_small.png, which you downloaded from this book's companion Web site and copied into the site's development_files folder. Select the file, and click Open (Windows) or Import to Library (Mac).

In the Fireworks PNG Import Settings dialog that appears, set the following options:

File Structure: Import as movie clip and retain layers

Objects: Keep all paths editable

Text: Either choice will work in this instance because all the text in the logo has been converted to vector paths to avoid font issues.

Do not check the Import as a single flattened bitmap check box.

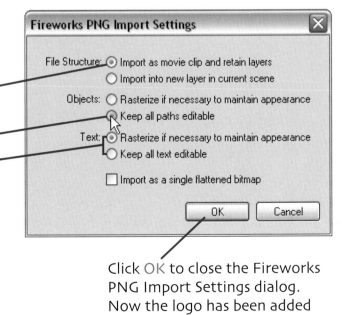

Click OK to close the Fireworks PNG Import Settings dialog. Now the logo has been added to the Library.

design the layout of your stage

organize symbols

If the Library panel for your file is not visible, choose Window > Library. In the Library panel, you'll see three new listings—two bitmaps (which were included in the logo file) and a folder named Fireworks Objects that contains the new logo symbol. Let's take a moment to begin organizing our symbols, which will save us time and headaches later.

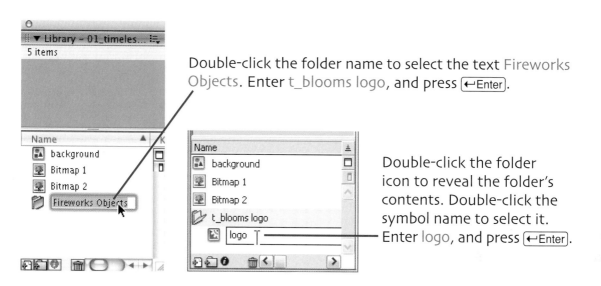

Double-click the folder name to select the text Fireworks Objects. Enter t_blooms logo, and press ←Enter.

Double-click the folder icon to reveal the folder's contents. Double-click the symbol name to select it. Enter logo, and press ←Enter.

Shift-click to select the two bitmap symbols in the Library panel. Click and drag the symbols into the t_blooms logo folder. Double-click the t_blooms logo folder icon to collapse the folder view.

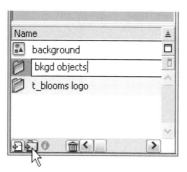

Click the New Folder button at the bottom of the Library panel to add a new folder to the list. Name the folder bkgd objects. Drag the other objects in the list into the new folder.

transform objects

Objects on your Stage, even symbols, can have different transformations applied to them. Transformations such as Scale, Rotate, and Skew are applied with the Free Transform tool. (See extra bits on Page 30.)

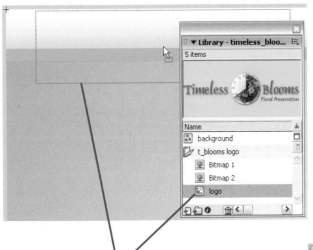

Confirm that you're still editing inside the background symbol. If not, double-click the symbol on the Stage to enter editing mode. Click to select the line & logo layer in the Timeline.

In the Library panel, navigate to the symbol we named logo. Click the symbol, and drag it onto the Stage near the top-left corner.

The logo is a bit bigger than we need, so we'll scale the instance down. With the instance still selected, choose the Free Transform tool. Eight transformation handles appear around the instance's bounding box.

Press and hold ⟨Alt⟩⟨Shift⟩ (Windows) or ⟨Option⟩⟨Shift⟩ (Mac). Click and drag the bottom-right transformation handle toward the center of the logo symbol instance. Release the mouse when Floral Preservation is just on top of the solid green background.

Choose the Selection tool to set the transformation.

design the layout of your stage

import bitmap image

With the logo placed and sized, we're going to balance the design by placing an image in the bottom-right corner of the Stage.

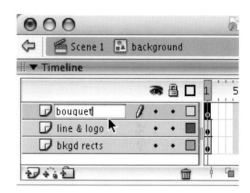

In the Timeline, add a new layer to your background symbol. Name the layer bouquet.

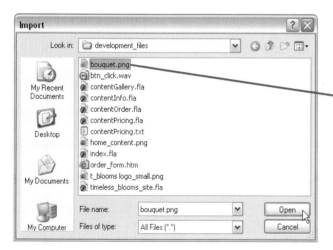

Choose File > Import > Import to Stage. In the Import dialog, navigate to the development_ files folder. Select the file bouquet.png, and click Open.

The bouquet image is placed on the Stage. Drag it to the bottom-right corner until only a little more than one fourth of the image is within the Stage area.

add masking layer

Having the bouquet image hanging off of the Stage won't affect the display of the final exported movie, but it is distracting as we continue developing the site. We'll use a Layer Mask to hide the unused parts.

Add a new layer and name it bouquet_mask.

Select the Rectangle tool. From the right edge of the Stage, above the image, drag out a rectangle that covers the area of the image that is on the Stage.

Right-click (Windows) or Ctrl-click (Mac) the layer bouquet_mask. Choose Mask from the drop-down menu.

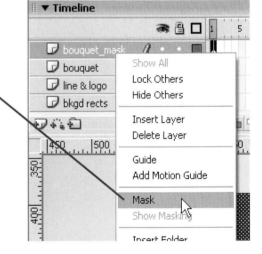

The overhanging part of the image is no longer visible!

Our background framework is complete, and now we're ready to add text. Save your file.

design the layout of your stage

extra bits

draw background p. 12

- In Flash, when an object is overlapping another, the overlapped section of the existing object is deleted. This makes adjustments such as nudging new objects into place a nightmare. To avoid this, you can either create a new layer for every object you draw or group an object as soon as you draw it. I prefer grouping.

reusable graphics p. 19

- Using symbols in Flash provides two main benefits: reduced file size and ease of editing.

  When you create a symbol and place instances of that symbol on the Stage, your movie's file size is reduced because no matter how many times you use it, the code required to define it is only included in the file once. Each instance just points to the symbol and describes any modifications to that symbol, such as transparency or size.

  Modifying work later is also much easier. Imagine that you've placed 100 blue squares (not instances of a blue square symbol) throughout your movie, and then you decide to change the color. You have to find and change all 100 squares. But if you made a symbol of a blue square and placed 100 instances, you only have to change the symbol, and the 100 instances are updated automatically.

design the layout of your stage

extra bits

edit a symbol p. 21

- When you have an object on the Stage that is a container for other objects (groups, symbols and text boxes) you can just double-click it to "get inside" and edit the contents.

- To exit the editing mode of the container, you can double-click outside the bounds of the container.

- Sometimes when you draw a line in Flash, it isn't placed at the top of the object stacking order like you'd expect it to be. Instead, it is placed behind other objects. Defying the standard convention that a new object is stacked above existing objects on the same layer, Flash stacks lines based on a mysterious formula involving the line's color that only programmers could come up with!

  You can do one of two things to make the line appear where you want it: group the line, which moves it to the top of the stack; or move the line to a layer above the current layer.

transform objects p. 26

- When you're scaling vector objects (those drawn in Flash or imported, as in the logo file) you can increase or decrease the size without negative effect. However, if you're working with a bitmap image, you'll want to avoid enlarging it. An enlarged bitmap has to be resampled and can become distorted or fuzzy. It's best to open the image in an image editor such as Adobe Photoshop or Macromedia Fireworks and scale it to the size you need.

design the layout of your stage

3. add and style text

With the graphic elements of the background in place, we can now add some text. We begin by adding and manipulating static text. (In later chapters we'll do more advanced things with text.) In this chapter we'll do the following:

Use text for graphic appeal.

Add and manipulate fixed-width text boxes.

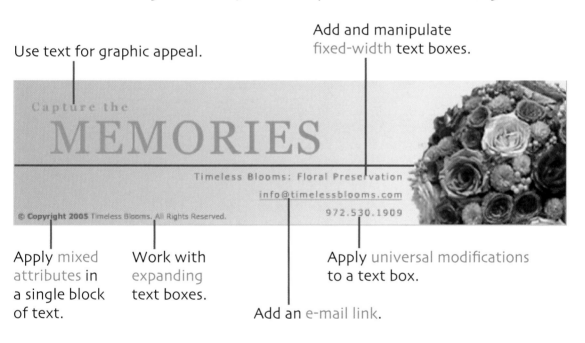

Apply mixed attributes in a single block of text.

Work with expanding text boxes.

Apply universal modifications to a text box.

Add an e-mail link.

add a single line of text

First we'll add company and copyright information to the background symbol so that it will be visible throughout the site.

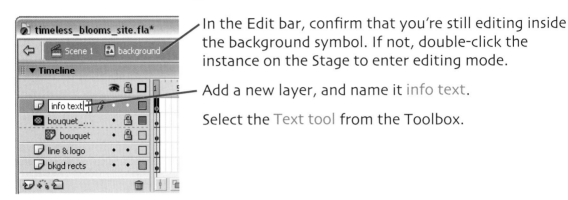

In the Edit bar, confirm that you're still editing inside the background symbol. If not, double-click the instance on the Stage to enter editing mode.

Add a new layer, and name it info text.

Select the Text tool from the Toolbox.

In the Property Inspector, set attributes as follows:

Click the Text (Fill) color control, and choose our dark green color from the Color pop-up pane.

Choose Static Text from the Text Type menu.

Select Verdana for the Font.

Enter 10 for Font Size.

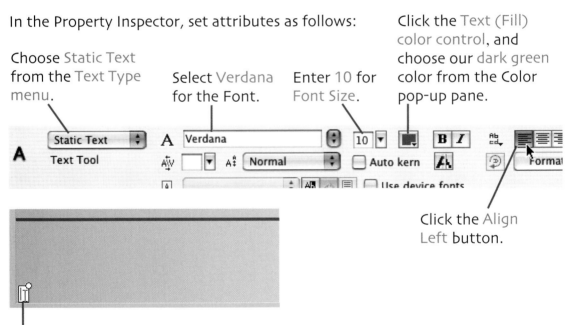

Click the Align Left button.

Click the Text tool in the bottom-left corner of the Stage. An empty text box with a blinking insertion point appears. The round Resize handle denotes that the text box does not have a fixed width and will expand horizontally to hold all the text entered.

© Copyright 2005 Timeless Blooms. All Rights Reserved.

Type © Copyright 2005 Timeless Blooms. All Rights Reserved.

Click on the Stage to close the text box.

Let's change the attributes of some of the text in this text box to add emphasis to the copyright notice.

Choose the Selection tool from the Toolbox, and double-click the text box to edit the text inside. To select the text © Copyright 2005, click to the left of the copyright symbol and drag past the 5.

With the text now selected, click the Bold Style button in the Property Inspector.

fixed-width text

Click on the Stage to close and deselect the text box. In the Property Inspector, change the Font Size to 12, and click to deselect the Bold Style button.

With the Text tool selected, click and drag out a text box to the left of the bouquet image and just below the line.

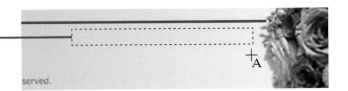

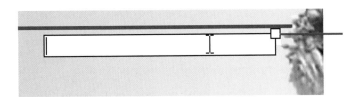

An empty text box appears. The square Resize handle denotes that the box has a fixed width, meaning text will wrap onto new lines rather than stay on one line and stretch the text box.

Enter Timeless Blooms: Floral Preservation. If the text wraps to a second line, click and drag the Resize handle until the text fits on one line.

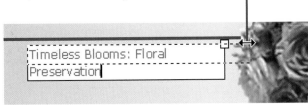

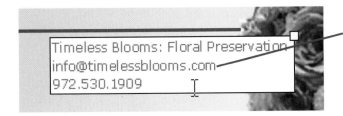

Press ⏎Enter, and type info@timelessblooms.com.

Press ⏎Enter, and type 972.530.1909.

Choose the Selection tool from the Toolbox to close the text box.

add and style text

change a text box

You can make universal changes to all of the text in a text box by selecting the box and making changes in the Property Inspector.

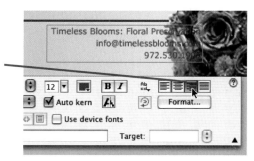

If the text box is not still selected, click it with the Selection tool. Click the Align Right button in the Property Inspector.

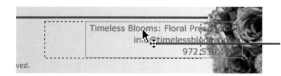

If some of your text is on top of the bouquet image, drag the text box to the left.

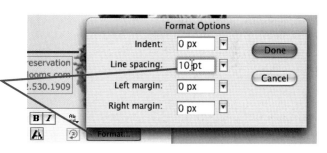

To spread out the lines of text, click the Format button on the Property Inspector. In the Format Options dialog, enter 10 for Line Spacing, and click OK.

Now let's spread the text out a bit. Enter 2 in the Property Inspector's Character Spacing text field.

If the last step caused the text on the first line to wrap, double-click the text box and drag out the Resize handle. Use the Selection tool to reposition the text box away from the bouquet.

add an e-mail link

We want contacting Timeless Blooms to be convenient for viewers of the Web site. Let's add a link to the e-mail address that will automatically launch a new e-mail message in the viewer's e-mail application.

Select the Text tool, and click inside the text box to open the box for editing. Select the text info@timelessblooms. com.

Choose Edit > Copy to copy the e-mail address to the clipboard.

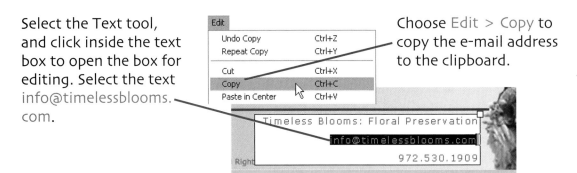

In the Property Inspector's URL Link field type mailto: and then paste the e-mail address into the field. Make sure there is no space between the colon and the pasted address.

Press ←Enter to set the URL attribute.

The standard convention on the Web is that clickable text is underlined. A dashed line appears under the e-mail address, but this is only a visual clue inside the Flash authoring environment that the text has a link; it won't be visible in the exported movie.

We need to add an underline that will display in our movie. Flash doesn't provide an Under-line style for text, so we'll create our own. With the Line tool, draw a line below the address. Set the line height to .25, and apply the medium green color to it.

add and style text

add graphic text

As our final step in designing the background of our Stage, we need to add a little more text. Unlike the other text we'll have in the site, this text serves a graphic purpose rather than informational—it conveys the theme of the business that this Web site promotes.

Choose the Text tool, and set the following attributes in the Property Inspector:

Color: Light Rose

Font: Georgia   Size: 16   Style: Bold

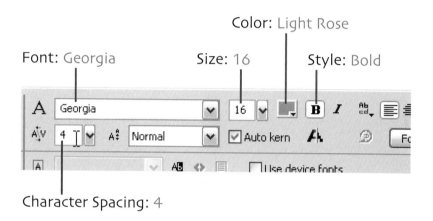

Character Spacing: 4

Click on the Stage, and type Capture the.

Click on the Stage to close and deselect the text box.

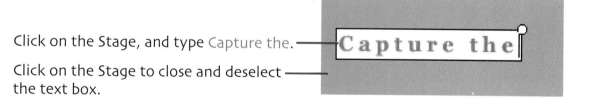

In the Property Inspector, set the Font Size to 64. Click the Bold Style button to deselect it.

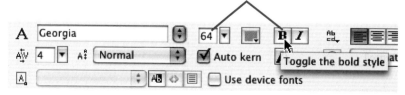

add graphic text (cont.)

Click the Stage to create another text box and type MEMORIES.

With the Selection tool, position the two text blocks so that they approximate the arrangement shown here.

In the Edit bar above the Stage, click Scene 1 to exit symbol-editing mode.

Save your file.

Our Stage's background is now complete, and we can begin working on the sections and animations in our site.

add and style text

4. use the timeline to organize your site

As you've probably guessed, the Timeline is used for animation in your Flash movie. But it also serves other purposes.

A frame can represent not only a fluid moment in an animation as an object slides across the Stage, but also a static point in the movie to which we navigate within our movie. In Flash development we use frames for animation, as reference points, and as organizational tools to ease development.

In this chapter, we learn the basics of working with different types of frames, naming frames for easy reference, and controlling frame playback. We'll learn to:

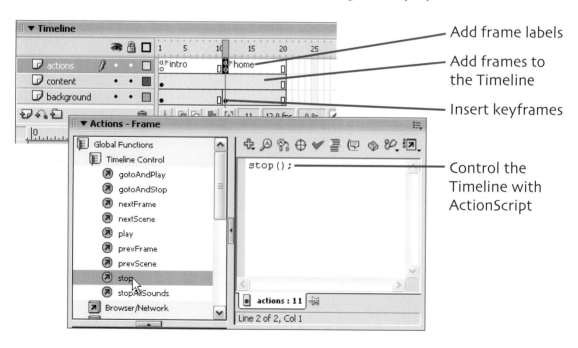

Add frame labels

Add frames to the Timeline

Insert keyframes

Control the Timeline with ActionScript

create the home page

Our home page is looking a little bare. Before we move on to working with frames, let's add some content.

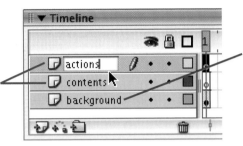

In the Timeline, rename the existing layer background.

Add one new layer named contents and another layer named actions.

From the vertical ruler on the left of the Stage, drag out a guide—lining it up with the 12 o'clock position on the clock in our logo.

Click the contents layer to make it the active layer.

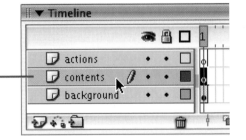

Choose File > Import > Import to Stage. In the Import dialog, navigate to the development_files folder. Select the file home_content.png, and click Open.

In the Fireworks PNG Import Settings dialog that appears, set the following options:

File Structure: Import as movie clip and retain layers

Objects: Keep all paths editable

Text: Either choice will work in this instance because there is no text in the file.

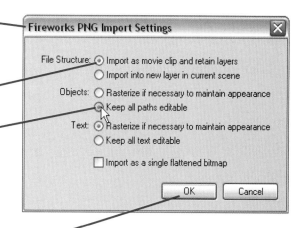

Click OK. The image appears on the Stage.

With the Selection tool, drag the graphic into place, aligning the first line of text with the vertical guide.

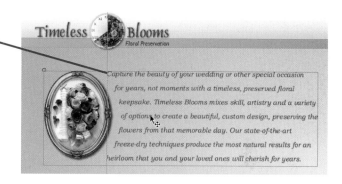

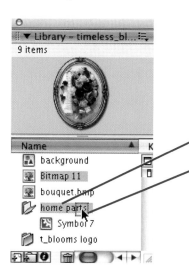

In the Library panel, rename the Fireworks Objects folder home parts. Double-click the folder to expand it.

Drag the bitmap symbol of the framed bouquet into the home parts folder.

Rename the movie clip symbol home content.

To save time and space, I won't instruct you to organize symbols throughout the rest of this book. However, keep in mind the organizing techniques we covered in Chapter 2.

add frames

Currently we have only one frame in our movie. The frames that you see in the Timeline now are available frames, but they're not yet defined. We'll define more frames to help us organize our movie and prepare it for adding animations in the next chapter. (See extra bits on Page 49.)

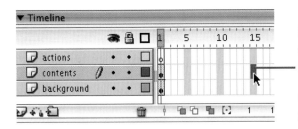

In the Timeline for the contents layer, click the empty cell beneath the 15 marker in the Timeline Header.

Choose Insert > Timeline > Frame, or press F5.

Notice four things:

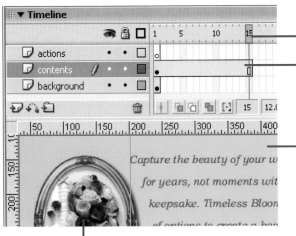

The Playhead has moved to display Frame 15.

Flash has automatically created frames 2 through 14.

Our background is not visible.

The contents of the layer's keyframe at Frame 1 are displayed now in Frame 15.

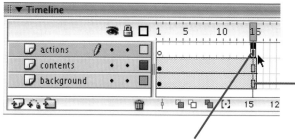

We have no background because Frame 15 has not been defined for the background layer. Add the frame now, repeating the steps you took to create the frame for the contents layer.

Insert Frame 15 for the actions layer.

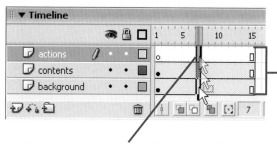

We now have 15 frames in all of our layers. Let's add five more frames to all the layers at once.

In the actions layer, click one of the frames and drag down to the background layer, selecting the frame in all three layers. Choose Insert > Timeline > Frame five times, or press F5 five times.

insert keyframes

Now we're going to add keyframes, which will let us change content from one point in the Timeline to another.

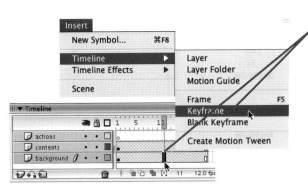

Click Frame 11 in the background layer, and choose Insert > Timeline > Keyframe.

We do this because later we're going to add an animated background that plays when our movie first loads. Keyframe 1 will contain the animated background, and Keyframe 11 will contain the static background we've already created.

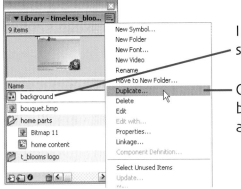

In the Library panel, select the symbol background.

On the right of the panel's title bar, click the Options menu icon, and choose Duplicate.

In the Duplicate Symbol dialog that appears, name the symbol animated background.

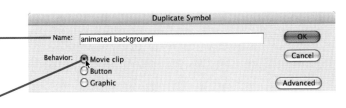

Choose Movie Clip for the Behavior, and click OK.

The animated background will have most of the same objects in the same place as the regular background, so we want the two different symbols to be placed identically. We can ensure this by swapping symbols.

Click Frame 1 in the Timeline
Header to move the Playhead to
Frame 1, or click and drag the
Playhead to Frame 1.

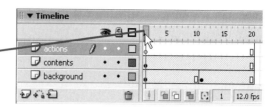

With the Selection tool, click on the Stage to select the background
symbol. (Click outside the bounds of the home content symbol so you
don't select it by mistake.)

Click the Swap Symbol button in
the Property Inspector.

In the Swap Symbol dialog,
select animated background,
and click OK.

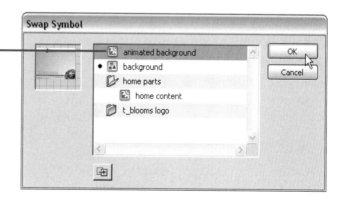

In the Property Inspector, click
the Symbol Behavior drop-down
menu, and choose Movie Clip.

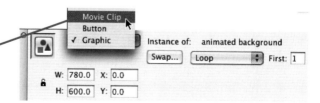

use the timeline to organize your site

add frame labels

Frame labels let you name frames for logical reference.
(See extra bits on Page 50.)

In the Timeline, click Keyframe 1 of
the actions layer.

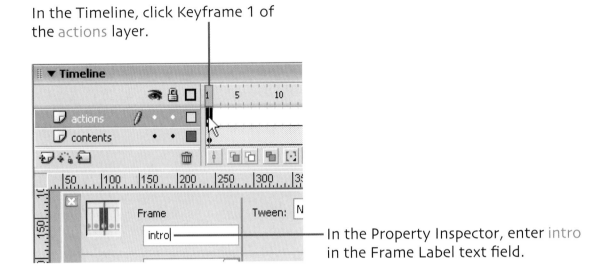

In the Property Inspector, enter intro
in the Frame Label text field.

Note that Keyframe 1 in the Timeline now displays a flag signifying that it has a
label. Also, because this keyframe has a span of 9 more frames, Flash has room
to display the frame label in the Timeline.

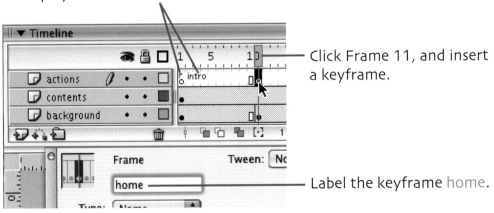

Click Frame 11, and insert
a keyframe.

Label the keyframe home.

control the timeline

By default, the Playhead in a Flash movie plays through all the frames in a time-line and loops endlessly unless you tell it otherwise. We use Actions applied to frames and buttons to control the Playhead. (See extra bits on Page 50.)

We'll stop the Playhead in keyframe intro by adding a Stop Action.

If the Actions panel is not visible, choose
Window > Development Panels > Actions.

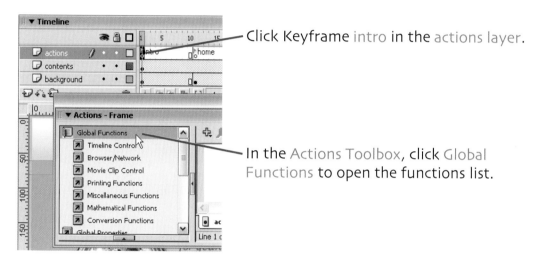

Click Keyframe intro in the actions layer.

In the Actions Toolbox, click Global Functions to open the functions list.

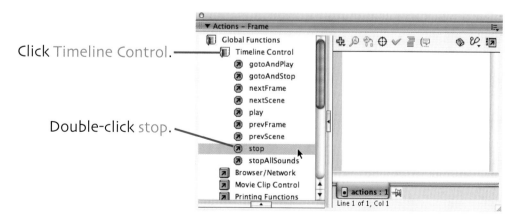

Click Timeline Control.

Double-click stop.

control the timeline (cont.)

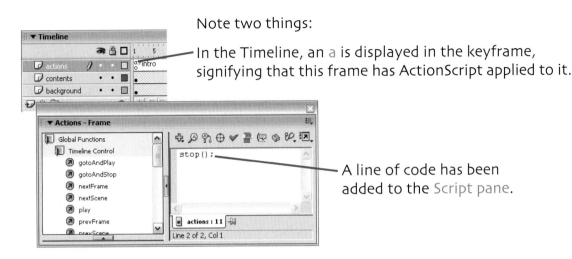

Note two things:

In the Timeline, an a is displayed in the keyframe, signifying that this frame has ActionScript applied to it.

A line of code has been added to the Script pane.

Congratulations! You've just used ActionScript to control your movie!

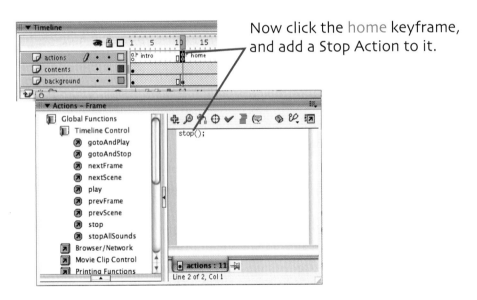

Now click the home keyframe, and add a Stop Action to it.

Save your file.

use the timeline to organize your site

extra bits

add frames p. 42

- Every Flash movie contains multiple timelines. Every scene has a main Timeline, and each symbol has its own independent Timeline, as you saw when editing our background. Within a scene or symbol, each layer also has its own Timeline. In complex Flash movies like the one we're building, it is best to use the scene's main Timeline for organizational and reference purposes only. Use the timelines available inside symbols for animation.

  We define two kinds of frames in a Timeline—basic frames and keyframes. Keyframes are where we do all of our work. Whenever you want to manually change the contents of a frame, you must do it in a keyframe. Basic frames make up what is known as a keyframe's span—the frames between that keyframe and the next. Frames act merely as clones of the preceding keyframe.

- By default, the first frame in any Timeline is a keyframe.

- If you change an object in a frame, you're actually making that change to the keyframe and all frames in its span. It can be incredibly painful to make a change in a particular frame, thinking that you're only changing that frame, and 30 minutes later realize you actually changed 15 frames, so be careful that you are always editing in a keyframe.

- In the Timeline, keyframes are marked with a bullet. A solid bullet signifies that the keyframe has contents, and a hollow bullet signifies an empty keyframe. The final frame in a keyframe span is marked with a hollow rectangle.

extra bits

add frame labels p. 46

- When you're working with multiple timelines throughout your movie, moving objects from place to place, and adding or removing frames as you work, it can be difficult to remember what frame number holds an object you're looking for or want to link to from elsewhere in the movie.

  If you have objects on a keyframe at Frame 70 but then add 8 frames to the Timeline, your keyframe is now at 78. If buttons or other movie clips are linking to that keyframe by number, you have to remember to search them out and change the link from 70 to 78. But if you've labeled the keyframe important_frame, that doesn't change, and all the pointers in your movie are still correct.

- It's a common practice in Flash development to add frames after a keyframe just to make enough room to display the frame label, making it easy to locate frames during development. In our Timeline so far, the only frames that will actually be seen by viewers are frames 1 and 11; the other frames will be bypassed. You'll understand this more when we add animations and navigation controlled with ActionScript later in the book.

control the timeline p. 47

- ActionScript is Flash's powerful scripting language that allows developers to control playback, establish complex interactions, and even develop Flash-based applications. While it is considered an easy language to use, those of us who are not programmers don't necessarily think so.

- In this book we'll avoid too much scripting by using very simple Actions (chunks of ActionScript) and Behaviors (prepackaged Actions) to control our timelines and provide navigation.

- To help keep us organized, we add an empty layer named actions to each of our timelines—using the layer only for labeling and Action-Script. This helps us keep the mechanics of our movie separate from the content and lets us visually track frame properties easily.

use the timeline to organize your site

5. add animation to your web site

By now you might be thinking "Enough with the boring stuff. I want to make things fly across the Stage." If that's the case, then you're going to love this chapter. Here we add the pizzazz to our Web site that separates it from an ordinary HTML-based site. In the following pages we'll do the following:

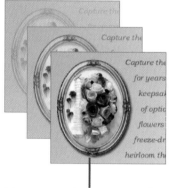

Add a Transition effect to make the bouquet image fade-in slowly at just the right moment

Pause playback of our movie using ActionScript

Add a Behavior to move the Playhead from one frame to another

Use a motion tween for a subtle fade-in of our content

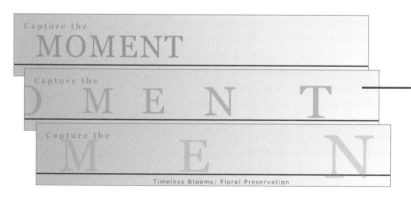

Use Timeline Effects to build a complex animation where text zooms in and out, changing words as it goes

create a motion

We sometimes use animation in subtle ways, rather than hit the viewer over the head with our brilliance. In this step, we'll create a very short fade-in of our home page's content. We do this so that when our movie loads, the content doesn't just pop onto the screen. We see this technique often on web sites and don't even realize there's animation, we just experience a smooth reveal of the contents.

To create the animation, we set up our content's beginning state and ending state, and then instruct Flash to create, or tween, the intermediate frames. (See extra bits on Page 77.)

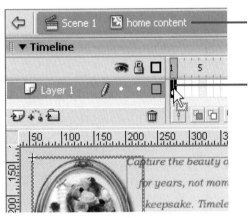

With the Selection tool, double-click the home content symbol to edit it.

In the Timeline, click Keyframe 1 of Layer 1 to select all of its contents—the image and the text. Choose Modify > Convert to Symbol, or press F8.

In the Convert to Symbol dialog, name the symbol fade contents, and choose the Graphic behavior. Click OK.

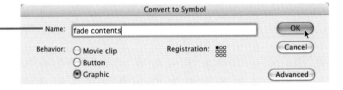

Insert a keyframe in Frame 12 (Insert > Timeline > Keyframe).

Click to select Keyframe 1.

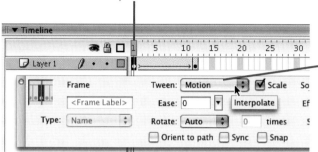

In the Property Inspector, click the Interpolation drop-down menu (labeled Tween), and choose Motion.

Notice in the Timeline that an arrow is displayed from Keyframe 1 to Keyframe 12, signifying an applied tween.

The symbol appears to be selected, but the Property Inspector is displaying the frame properties, not the symbol. Click the symbol to change the contents of the Property Inspector.

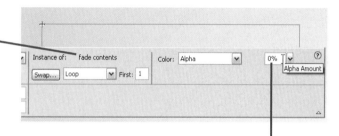

In the Property Inspector, click the Color Styles drop-down menu, and choose Alpha. Set the Alpha Amount to 0%. The symbol is no longer visible.

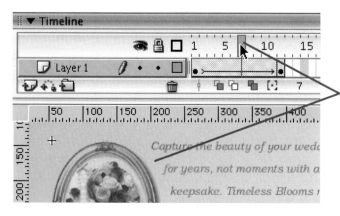

Move the Playhead to a couple of different frames between 1 and 12 and notice the incremental changes in transparency.

That's it. You just created your first tweened animation.

add animation to your web site   **53**

play animation in flash

You can preview an animation inside the Flash application. Let's watch the animation we just created. Choose Control > Play, or press (←Enter).

You may think the animation is a bit jerky. This happens when there are too many frames in an animation and the eye is able to distinguish too many of the individual static images. Let's shorten the animation to make that less noticeable.

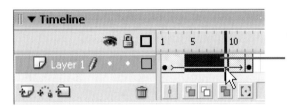

In the Timeline, click a frame and drag to the right—selecting approximately 6 frames. Be sure you don't drag past Frame 11 and select the keyframe.

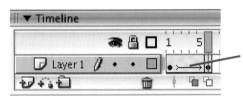

Choose Edit > Timeline > Remove Frames, or press (Shift)(F5). The animation is shortened, and Flash re-interpolates the tweened frames.

Press (←Enter) to view the animation now. You should see an appreciably smoother animation.

Remember that the Playhead loops endlessly unless you tell it otherwise. To make this animation play only once, do the following:

1 Add a new layer to the Timeline, and name it actions.

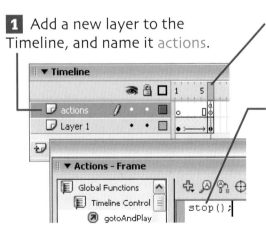

2 Insert a keyframe at the same frame position as the final keyframe in the animation. If you deleted 6 frames, it will be Frame 6.

3 In the Actions panel, enter stop(); in the Script pane, or add the action using the steps we used previously.

4 Click Scene 1 in the Edit bar, or double-click the Stage to exit symbol-editing mode.

complex animation

As easy as creating the tweened animation was, Flash goes one major step further. Timeline Effects allow quick and easy creation of some of the most common animation techniques developers want to create.

We'll use a series of Timeline Effects to create an animated introduction in which our graphic text zooms in and out, changing from Capture the Love to Capture the Moment and finally to Capture the Memories. (See extra bits on Page 77.)

In Keyframe 1 of the background layer, double-click the animated background symbol to edit it.

In the Layers column of the Timeline, select the info text layer. Add two new layers. Name the first layer animated text and the second actions.

In Keyframe 1 of the info text layer, select the MEMORIES text box. Choose Edit > Cut to move the text to the clipboard. Select the animated text layer, and choose Edit > Paste in Place.

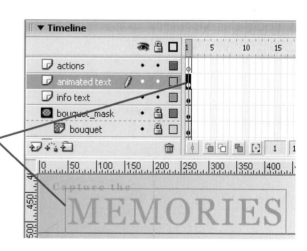

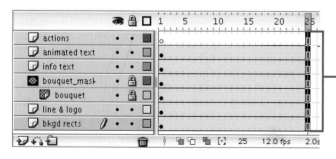

In the actions layer, click Frame 25, and drag down to layer bkgd rects, selecting the frame in all of the layers. Press F5 to add frames to the layers.

complex animation (cont.)

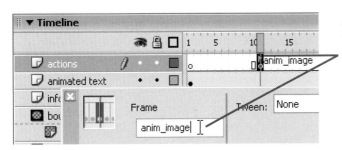

Add a keyframe in Frame 11 of the actions layer, and label the frame anim_image.

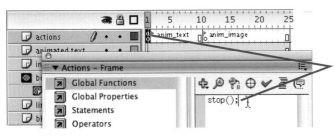

Select Keyframe 1, and enter stop(); in the Actions panel Script pane. In the Property Inspector, label the frame anim_text.

1 In Frame 11 of the animated text layer, add a keyframe.

2 Move the Playhead back to the anim_text keyframe.

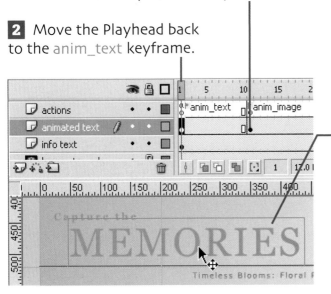

3 Select the MEMORIES text box.

Choose Modify > Convert to Symbol, or press F8. In the Convert to Symbol dialog, name the symbol text anima-tion. Select Movie Clip as the Behavior, and click OK.

Double-click the new symbol to edit it. Add three layers to the Timeline. Rename Layer 4 actions. We won't worry about naming the other layers because Flash renames layers when you apply Timeline Effects.

We want a slight delay in our movie before the animation starts. With our movie's frame rate of 12 frames per second, we can create a one second delay by starting our animation on Frame 13.

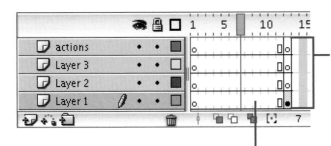

Click Frame 13 in the actions layer, and drag down to Layer 1, selecting the frame in all four layers. Choose Modify > Timeline > Convert to Keyframes, or press F6 .

Move the Playhead to any of the previous frames, and delete the MEMORIES text box from Layer 1—deleting it from Keyframe 1's entire span.

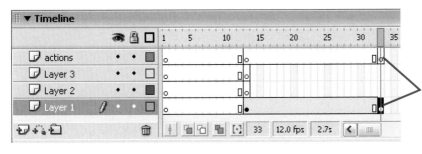

Each segment of our animation is going to be 20 frames long. So let's skip to Frame 33 and insert keyframes in the actions layer and Layer 1 for the start of our second segment.

copy and paste frames

Let's copy the text from Layer 1 to the other layers to set up our animation.

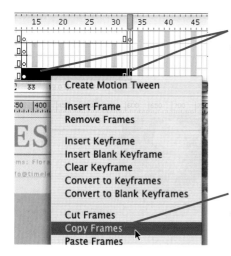

Select Frame 13 in Layer 1. ⟨Shift⟩-click Frame 33 to select the range of frames.

Right-click (Windows) or ⟨Control⟩-click (Mac), and choose Copy Frames from the drop-down menu.

Select Frame 13 in Layer 2. Right-click (Windows) or ⟨Control⟩-click (Mac) and choose Paste Frames. Select Frame 13 in Layer 3, and paste the frames again.

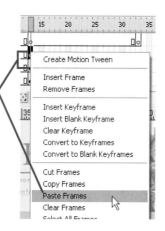

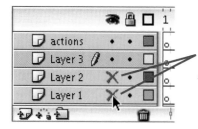

In the Layers column of the Timeline, click in the Eye column in Layer 1 and Layer 2 to hide them. A red X should appear in the column to signify the layers are hidden.

add timeline effects

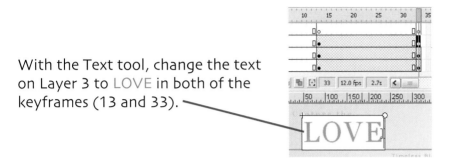

With the Text tool, change the text on Layer 3 to LOVE in both of the keyframes (13 and 33).

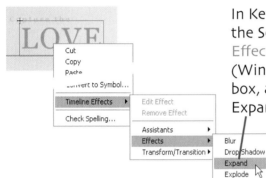

In Keyframe 13, select the LOVE text box with the Selection tool. Choose Insert > Timeline Effects > Effects > Expand, or right-click (Windows) or Control-click (Mac) on the text box, and choose Timeline Effects > Effects > Expand from the drop-down menu.

1 In the Expand dialog, select Squeeze for the Expand Style.

2 Click the Update Preview button, and note the change in the animation.

3 Enter 200 for the Fragment Offset value.

4 Set the values for Change Fragment Size by to 120 for Height and 110 for Width.

5 Click OK.

Press ⏎Enter to preview the animation. It's close to the effect we want, but the letters aren't moving quite far enough.

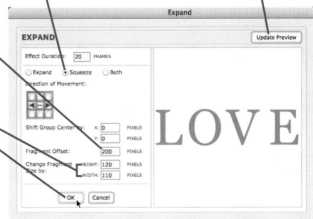

add timeline effects (cont.)

Move the Playhead back to Keyframe 13, and select the symbol that the effect created. (The original text box has been broken up into pieces; that's why we copied it into all of the other keyframes before we started adding the effects.)

In the Property Inspector, click the Edit button to launch the Expand dialog.

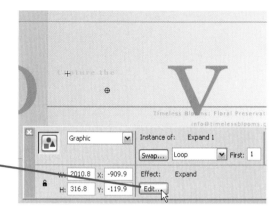

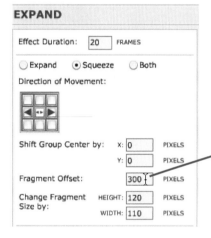

Change the Fragment Offset value to 300, and click OK.

With our animation set to our liking, we're going to add a motion tween of alpha transparency.

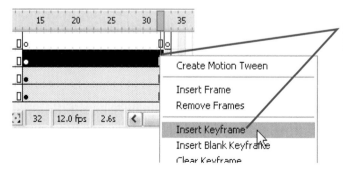

Select Frame 32, and insert a keyframe.

Read the warning dialog that appears, and click OK. We won't be able to make further changes to the animation.

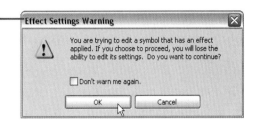

Move the Playhead back to Keyframe 13, and select the symbol. Click the Color Styles drop-down menu and select Alpha. Set the Alpha Amount to 10%.

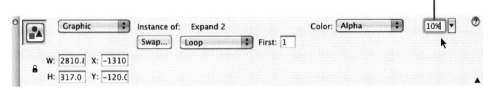

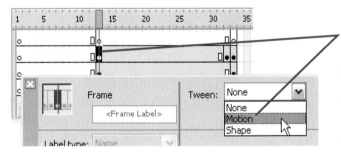

In the Timeline, click Keyframe 13 to select it. In the Property Inspector, click the Interpolation drop-down menu and choose Motion.

Press ⏎Enter to preview the animation.

That completes the zoom-in of the text.
Now let's do a reverse, and zoom the text out.

add animation to your web site

add timeline effects (cont.)

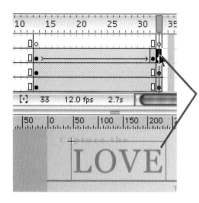

Move the Playhead to Keyframe 33 and select the LOVE text box. Right-click (Windows) or Control-click (Mac) on the text box, and choose Timeline Effects > Effects > Expand from the drop-down menu.

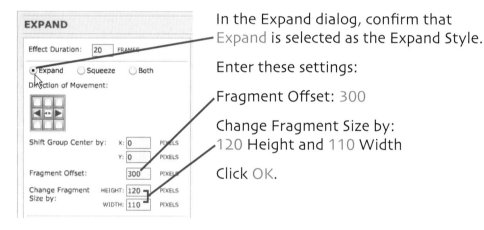

In the Expand dialog, confirm that Expand is selected as the Expand Style.

Enter these settings:

Fragment Offset: 300

Change Fragment Size by:
120 Height and 110 Width

Click OK.

Select Frame 52, and insert a keyframe. Click OK in the warning dialog.

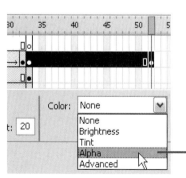

Click to select the symbol. In the Property Inspector, click the Color Styles drop-down menu, and choose Alpha. Set the Alpha Amount to 10%.

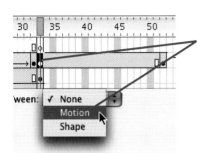

Select Keyframe 33, and set a Motion tween in the Property Inspector.

Move the Playhead to Keyframe 1, and press ←Enter to preview the animation.

You should see the text fade and zoom in and then fade and zoom out. If not, review the steps above.

With the animation of the word LOVE complete, we need to repeat the process to create a zoom for our next word: MOMENT.

In the Eye column of the Timeline, click to hide the current layer, and then click to show Layer 2.

Change the text in Layer 2 to MOMENT in keyframes 13 and 33.

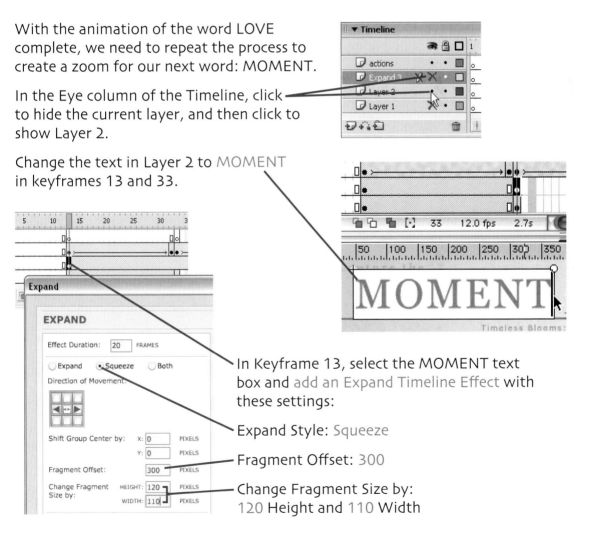

In Keyframe 13, select the MOMENT text box and add an Expand Timeline Effect with these settings:

Expand Style: Squeeze

Fragment Offset: 300

Change Fragment Size by:
120 Height and 110 Width

add timeline effects (cont.)

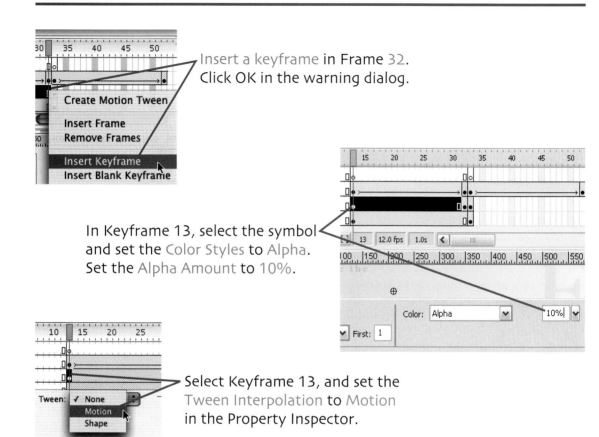

Insert a keyframe in Frame 32. Click OK in the warning dialog.

In Keyframe 13, select the symbol and set the Color Styles to Alpha. Set the Alpha Amount to 10%.

Select Keyframe 13, and set the Tween Interpolation to Motion in the Property Inspector.

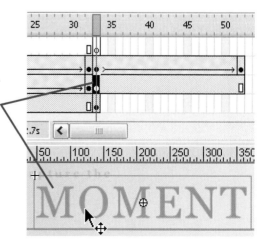

In Keyframe 33, select the MOMENT text box and add an Expand Timeline Effect with these settings:

Expand Style: Expand

Fragment Offset: 300

Change Fragment Size by: 120 Height and 110 Width

　add animation to your web site

Insert a keyframe in Frame 52.
Click OK in the warning dialog.

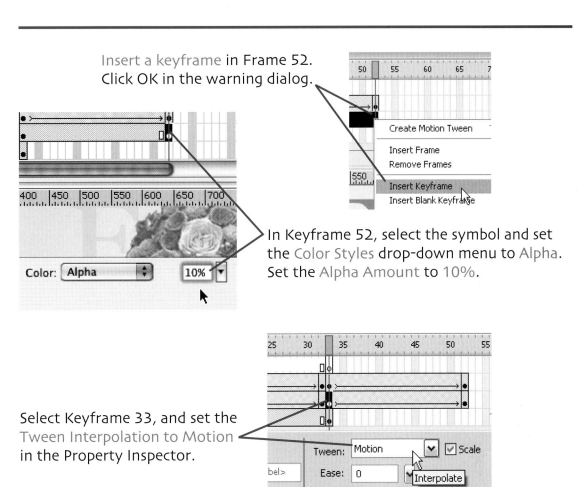

In Keyframe 52, select the symbol and set the Color Styles drop-down menu to Alpha. Set the Alpha Amount to 10%.

Select Keyframe 33, and set the Tween Interpolation to Motion in the Property Inspector.

That completes our second segment of animation. Now we just need to add a zoom in segment for our final word: MEMORIES.

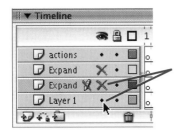

Hide the current layer and make Layer 1 visible.

In Keyframe 13, select the MEMORIES text box, and add an Expand Timeline Effect with these settings:

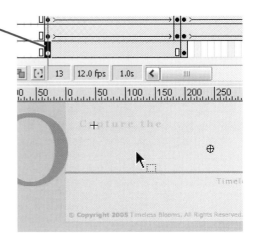

Expand Style: Squeeze

Fragment Offset: 300

Change Fragment Size by: 120 Height and 110 Width

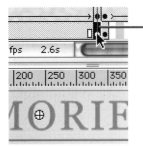

Insert a keyframe in Frame 32. Click OK in the warning dialog.

In Keyframe 13, select the symbol and set the Color Styles drop-down menu to Alpha. Set the Alpha Amount to 10%.

Select Keyframe 13, and set the Tween Interpolation to Motion in the Property Inspector.

move animations

Now all of our animation segments are created, but they're stacked on top of one another, all playing at the same time. We need to spread them out in the Timeline.

The animation for the word LOVE will stay where it is, playing in frames 13 through 52. We want the MOMENT animation to start about one second (12 frames) later, so we'll move its first frame to 64.

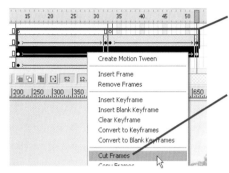

In the layer containing the MOMENT animation, click Keyframe 13. Press [Shift] and click Keyframe 52 to select the range of frames. Right-click (Windows) or [Control]-click (Mac) on the selected frames, and choose Cut Frames from the drop-down menu.

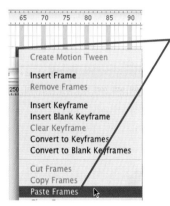

Right-click (Windows) or [Control]-click (Mac) on Frame 64, and choose Paste Frames from the drop-down menu.

Now let's move the MEMO-RIES animation to begin in Frame 115. In the layer containing the MEMORIES animation, select the range of frames from 13 to 33. Right-click (Windows) or [Control]-click (Mac) on the selected frames, and choose Cut Frames from the drop-down menu.

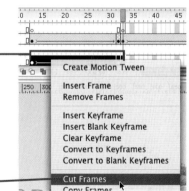

Right-click (Windows) or [Control]-click (Mac) on Frame 115, and choose Paste Frames from the drop-down menu.

Move the Playhead to Keyframe 1, and press [←Enter] to preview our complete animation.

pause an animation

The animation looks great, but it all flies by too fast. We want to add a pause after the text zooms in and before it zooms back out, holding the word in place long enough for it to register with the viewer. (See extra bits on Page 78.)

First we'll pause the word LOVE. Make all of the layers in the symbol visible. In the actions layer, select Frame 32 and, add a keyframe.

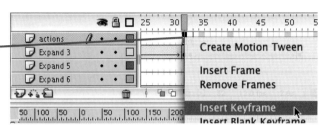

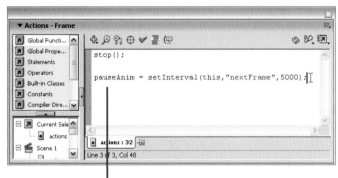

Open the Actions panel, and enter this code in the Script pane:

```
stop();
pauseAnim = setInterval(this,"nextFrame",5000);
```

This code stops the animation, creates a timer, and moves to the next frame after 5 seconds (5000 milliseconds).

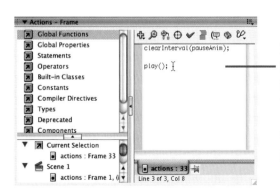

Select Keyframe 33 in the Timeline. Enter this code in the Script pane to delete the timer and play through the rest of the Timeline:

```
clearInterval(pauseAnim);
play();
```

add animation to your web site

Select Frame 34, and choose Insert >
Timeline > Insert Blank Keyframe.
This restricts the ActionScript to
Frame 33 only.

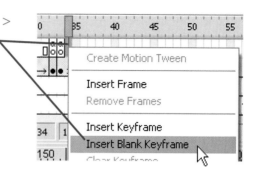

Next we'll pause the word MOMENT using the same ActionScript code.
In the actions layer, click to select Frame 32. [Shift]-click Frame 34 to select
all three keyframes.

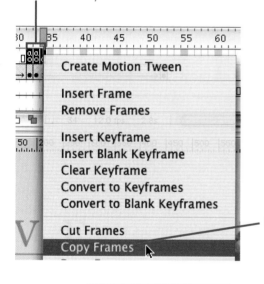

Copy the frames.

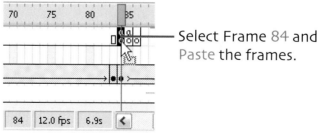

Select Frame 84 and
Paste the frames.

preview your movie

Up to this point, we've previewed our animations in the Flash workspace. To preview the effect of the ActionScript pause however, the animation has to be exported as a SWF file and viewed in the Flash Player.

We can do that quickly without going through the export process.

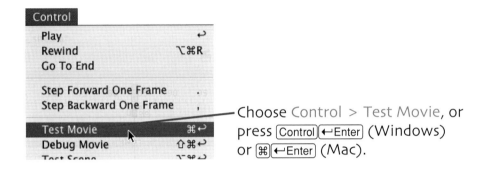

Choose Control > Test Movie, or press (Control)(←Enter) (Windows) or (⌘)(←Enter) (Mac).

Flash quickly exports the SWF, opens a new window, and plays the animation.

Notice the pause on the words LOVE and MOMENT; our ActionScript is working.

The animation loops because we haven't set any ActionScript in the final frame of the Timeline. We'll do that next.

Click the Close button to close the Flash Player window.

control movie clips

Remember that our text animation movie clip is playing in Keyframe 1 of the animated background movie clip. That frame, labeled anim_text, has Action-Script that stopped the Playhead. We're going to move the Playhead forward with ActionScript in the final frame of the text animation movie.

Flash provides easy-to-use, pre-packaged actions called Behaviors. We'll use a Behavior to add the ActionScript we want.

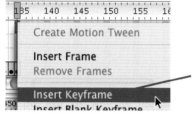 In the actions layer, add a keyframe to Frame 135.

Open the Behaviors panel (Window > Development Panels > Behaviors). Click the Add Behavior button.

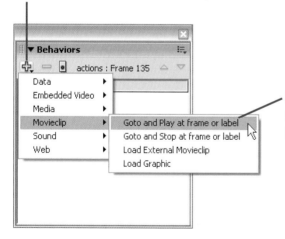 In the drop-down menu, choose Movieclip > Goto and Play at Frame or Label.

control movie clips (cont.)

In the Goto and Play at frame or label dialog, select (animated background) from the list.

Confirm that the button labeled Relative is selected.

In the Frame Number or Frame Label text field, enter anim_image.

Goto and Play at frame or label

Choose the movie clip that you want to begin playing:

this._parent

- _root
  - (animated background)
    - (logo)
    - (text animation)

( ) Relative   ( ) Absolute

Enter the frame number or frame label at which the movie clip should start playing. To start from the beginning, type '1':

anim_image

OK   Cancel

Click OK.

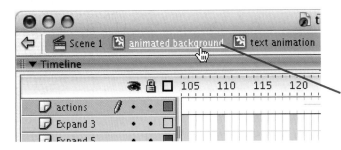

Our text animation is now complete. Click animated background in the Edit Bar to exit symbol-editing mode on the text animation movie clip.

add a transition effect

As the final piece in our intro animation, we want the image of the bouquet to appear after the text animation completes. We'll use a Transition effect to fade it in.

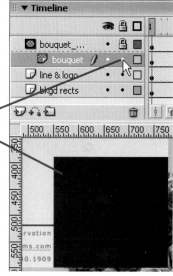

In the Layers column of the Timeline panel, click the Lock icon in the bouquet layer to unlock it. The rectangle we used to mask the bouquet image becomes visible when either layer is unlocked. Ignore it for now. Hide the bouquet_mask layer.

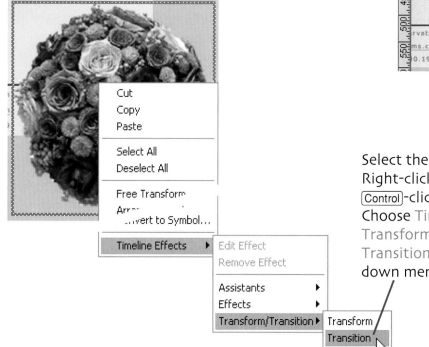

Select the bouquet image. Right-click (Windows) or [Control]-click (Mac) the image. Choose Timeline Effects > Transform/Transition > Transition in the drop-down menu.

add a transition effect

1 In the Transition dialog, enter a value of 15 frames for the Effect Duration.

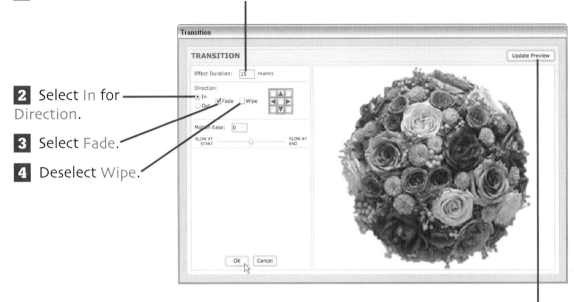

2 Select In for Direction.

3 Select Fade.

4 Deselect Wipe.

5 Click the Update Preview button to preview the changes.

6 Click OK.

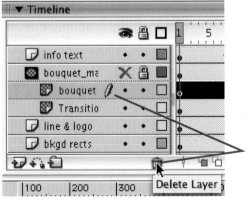

Flash has created a new layer in the Timeline and placed the transition there, leaving the layer bouquet empty. Let's delete it. Select the bouquet layer. Click the Delete Layer button at the bottom-right of the layers column.

Now we need to move the transition so that it begins after the text animation ends. In the transition layer, click any frame between 1 and 15; the range of frames containing the transition is selected.

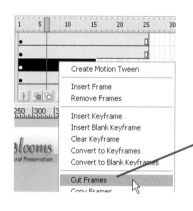

Right-click (Windows) or [Control]-click (Mac) the selected frames, and choose Cut Frames from the drop-down menu. Click OK in the warning dialog that appears.

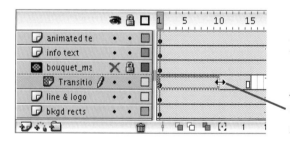

Move the cursor over Frame 15, the final frame in the span from Keyframe 1. Press [Ctrl] (Windows) or ⌘ (Mac). A bi-directional arrow cursor appears. Click and drag the frame to the left, stopping in Frame 10.

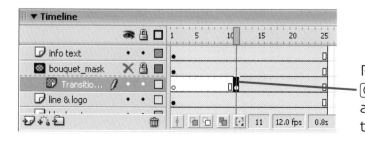

Right-click (Windows) or [Control]-click (Mac) Frame 11, and choose Paste Frames from the drop-down menu.

add a transition effect

Make the bouquet_mask layer visible again. Lock the transition layer.

Our final step in creating the intro animation is to have its last frame move the Playhead in the main Timeline to the frame with the static background.

Add a keyframe in Frame 25 of the actions layer.

Open the Behaviors panel. Click the Add Behavior button.

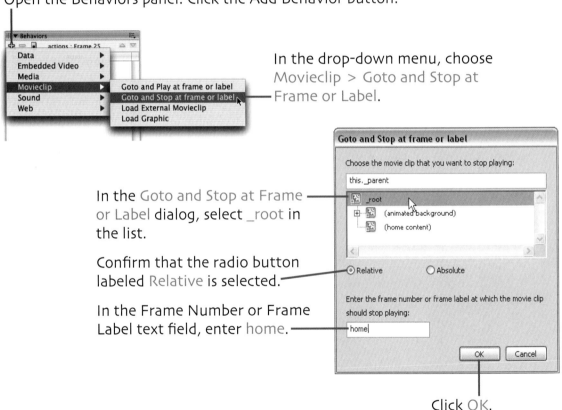

In the drop-down menu, choose Movieclip > Goto and Stop at Frame or Label.

In the Goto and Stop at Frame or Label dialog, select _root in the list.

Confirm that the radio button labeled Relative is selected.

In the Frame Number or Frame Label text field, enter home.

Click OK.

Click Scene 1 in the Edit Bar to exit symbol-editing mode. Save your file.

That's it. Our intro animation is complete. Press ⌈Control⌉⌈←Enter⌉ (Windows) or ⌘⌈←Enter⌉ (Mac) to preview your work in the Flash Player window.

extra bits

create a motion p. 52

- An animation is a series of static images (frames), where objects change incrementally from a beginning point to an end point. In Flash, we can define the beginning and end states with keyframes and let Flash generate the incremental frames. This method of creating the in-between frames is called tweening.

- There are two types of tweens in Flash: motion and shape. Motion tween is a bit of a misnomer, as it can be used to create changes not only in placement (motion) but also in alpha transparency, size, rotation, skew, and color effect. Motion tweens are applied to keyframes in a layer and only work when the layer contains only groups, symbol instances, and/or text blocks.

  Shape tweens work on shapes, not groups, symbols, or text blocks, and are used to change or "morph" the appearance of the shape.

complex animation p. 55

- Ah, the Flash intro to a Web site—probably the most reviled Web phenomenon since the HTML Blink tag. The interminable wait to see the content you came to the site for in the first place and the frantic search for a Skip button, hoping the developer included one, made it all too much to bear and sent many viewers fleeing without ever getting into the site.

  So what will we do? Create an intro, of course! However, we're going to create one that's done the right way—the evolved way. Here are the rules we'll follow to ensure that the animation doesn't irritate our viewers and doesn't get in the way of our content, which is, after all, the reason for having the site. The guidelines and how we're following them are as follows:

  Make it simple and meaningful. Our animation will be elegant while actually furthering Timeless Blooms' marketing message of capturing the emotion of special events.

continues on next page

extra bits

Don't let your intro obscure real content and navigation. Allow users to "get on with it" without waiting for the intro to finish. Our content and navigation buttons will be available from Frame 1, and the animation occurs outside the main content area.

Once viewers have seen the animation, don't make them view it again when navigating back to the home page from other areas of the site. This is why we created two keyframes in our main Timeline and created two background symbols, one for the intro and one for home.

pause an animation p. 68

- You've already seen that you can add time between animations by adding blank frames. We could add frames between the animation segments here, but we want a five second pause, which would require adding 60 blank frames, and our Timeline is already long and unwieldy. Instead, we'll use ActionScript to pause the Timeline.

- As a beginning Flash developer without deep understanding of ActionScript or other programming languages, you can often find code examples to use without understanding the technicalities of what they do.

  There are many resources on the Web that provide such examples. Visit the Macromedia Developer Forums at www.macromedia. com/support/forums/. Also, you can type a question like "how to pause a movie in Flash" in a Web search engine like google.com and get pointers to multiple developer sites offering code help.

- The code we use in this step is very simple. You can copy and paste it into any of your projects to create a pause in animation. To change the amount of time, simply change the number. Time is in milliseconds (1000ths) so 5000 equals 5 seconds.

add animation to your web site

6. build a navigation system

So far, we've created a great looking home page with an engaging introductory animation. But the site doesn't have any real content yet. It's like a movie with opening credits but no scenes revealing the plot.

In this chapter, we add keyframes to the main Timeline to define the site's sections, and create interactive buttons to navigate between those sections.

create buttons

The Web site has five sections: Home, Info, Gallery, Pricing, and Order. We need to create a button for each section. (See extra bits on Page 100.)

Choose Insert > New Symbol, or press [Ctrl][F8] (Windows) or [⌘][F8] (Mac).

In the Create New Symbol dialog, enter btn_gallery, and choose Button for the Behavior. Click OK.

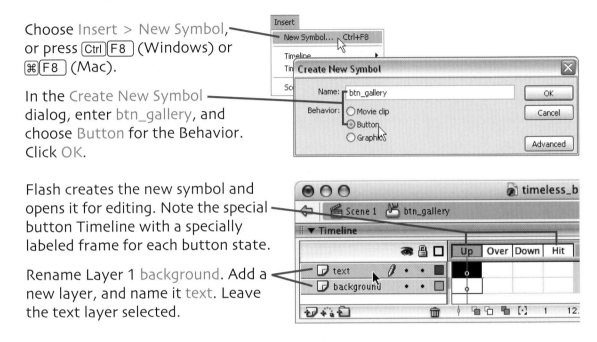

Flash creates the new symbol and opens it for editing. Note the special button Timeline with a specially labeled frame for each button state.

Rename Layer 1 background. Add a new layer, and name it text. Leave the text layer selected.

Click the Stage to reset the Property Inspector. Choose the Text tool, and set the following attributes in the Property Inspector:

Character Spacing: 0

Text Type: Static Text

Font: Verdana   Font Size: 14

Text (Fill) color: our light yellow

Alignment: Align Center

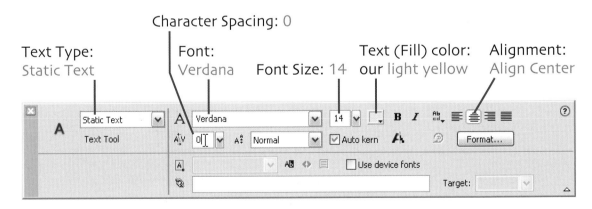

build a navigation system

Click near the Registration Point (+) in the center of the Stage, and type Gallery.

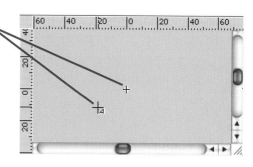

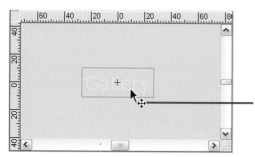

With the Selection tool, position the text box approximating the placement shown here.

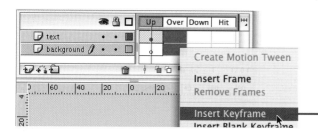

Our buttons won't have a background in the Up state, so we're ready to move on to creating the Over state. In the Timeline, select the Over frame in both layers, and insert a keyframe.

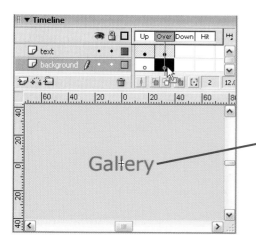

The Gallery text box has been copied into the Over frame. With the Selection tool, select the text box and change the color to our dark green.

Now we'll draw a circle for the background. Select the Over frame in the background layer.

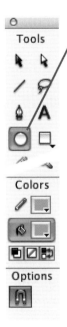

In the Tools panel, choose the Oval tool, and select our medium green color for both Stroke and Fill.

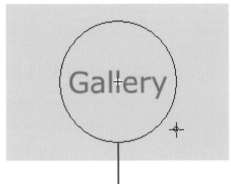

Before your click the Stage to draw the circle, press and hold [Alt] (Windows) or [Option] (Mac) to draw the circle from the middle, and press and hold [Shift] to constrain the oval to a circle.

Move the cursor over the Registration Point in the middle of the Stage. Click and drag out a circle slightly larger than the Gallery text. This completes the Over state.

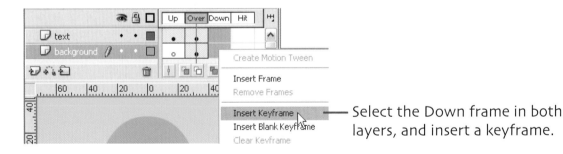

Select the Down frame in both layers, and insert a keyframe.

In the Layers column of the Timeline, click in the Eye column to hide the text layer.

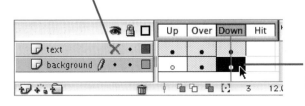

Select the Down frame in the background layer.

Select the Paint Bucket tool.

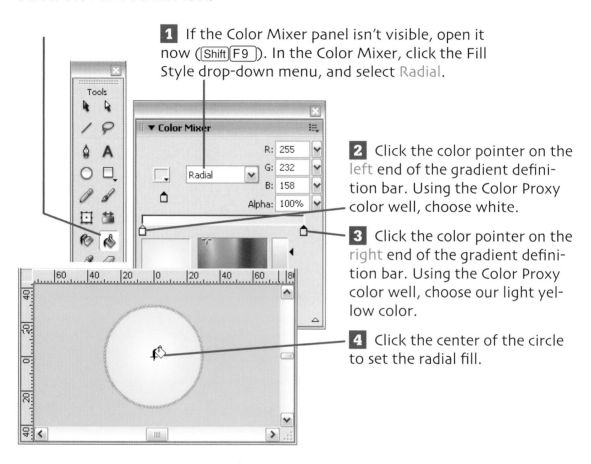

1 If the Color Mixer panel isn't visible, open it now (Shift F9). In the Color Mixer, click the Fill Style drop-down menu, and select Radial.

2 Click the color pointer on the left end of the gradient definition bar. Using the Color Proxy color well, choose white.

3 Click the color pointer on the right end of the gradient definition bar. Using the Color Proxy color well, choose our light yellow color.

4 Click the center of the circle to set the radial fill.

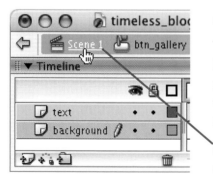

Make the text layer visible again.

The last step in creating a button is defining the Hit state, which defines the area of the button that responds to mouse activity. Before we do that, we're going to place the button on the Stage of our movie and then edit the button symbol in place.

Click Scene 1 in the Edit bar to exit symbol-editing mode.

create buttons (cont.)

Add a new layer to the Timeline, and name it buttons. Drag the layer to position it between the contents and actions layers.

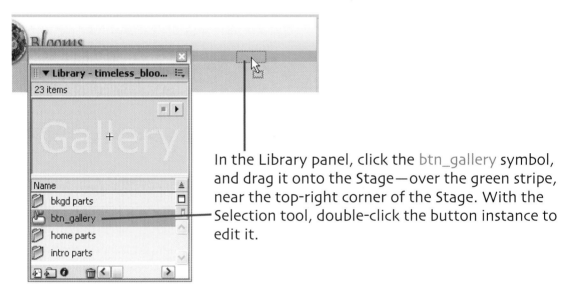

In the Library panel, click the btn_gallery symbol, and drag it onto the Stage—over the green stripe, near the top-right corner of the Stage. With the Selection tool, double-click the button instance to edit it.

Select the Hit frame in the background layer, and insert a keyframe.

The Hit area is defined by the shape of any objects in the frame. We only want a part of the circle to define our Hit area.

With the Selection tool, click and drag out a selection marquee to select the area of the circle that extends above the green stripe. Delete the selection. Repeat this procedure on the bottom section of the circle.

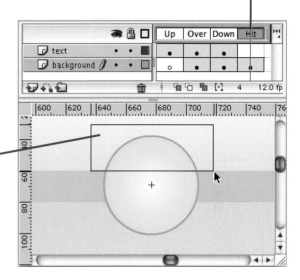

The remaining pieces of the circle now define our Hit area.

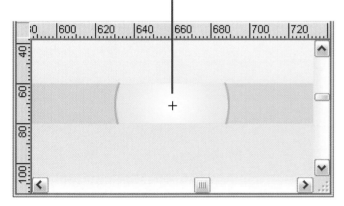

We've now completed a button design.

Click Scene 1 in the Edit bar to exit symbol-editing mode.

preview button actions

We can preview our button actions inside Flash.

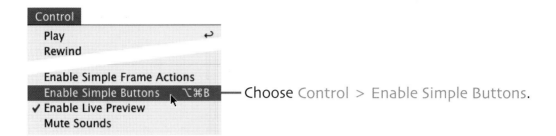

Choose Control > Enable Simple Buttons.

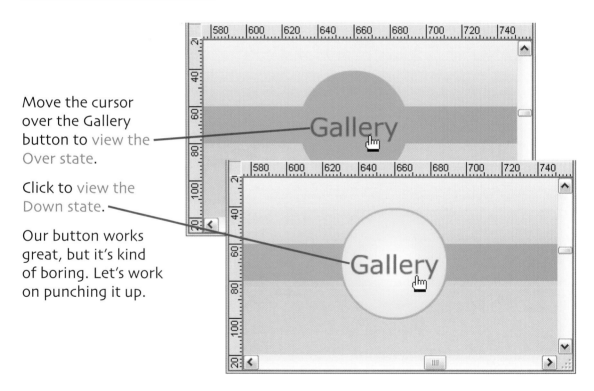

Move the cursor over the Gallery button to view the Over state.

Click to view the Down state.

Our button works great, but it's kind of boring. Let's work on punching it up.

Choose Control > Enable Simple Buttons again to turn off button preview.

animate a button state

To make our button more interesting, we're going to add a small animation to the Over state and add a slight offset to the Down state.

With the Selection tool, double-click the button instance to edit it.

In the Timeline, click the Down frame of the background layer to select the circle with the gradient fill. Copy the circle to the clipboard.

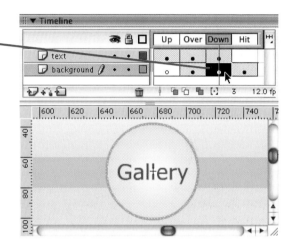

Click the Over frame of the background layer, selecting the solid green circle. Convert the selection to a symbol (F8). Name the symbol btn_anim, choose Movie Clip for the Behavior, and click the center Registration point.

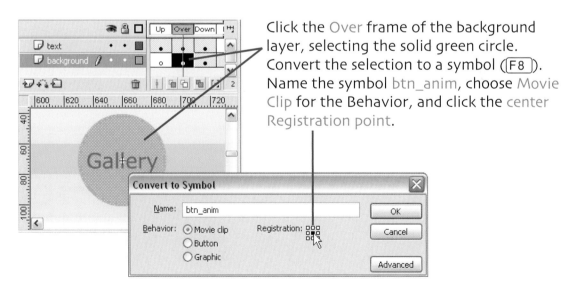

animate a button (cont.)

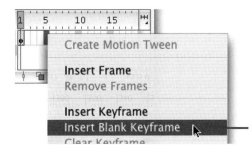

Double-click the new symbol to edit it. Insert a blank keyframe in Frame 5 of the Timeline.

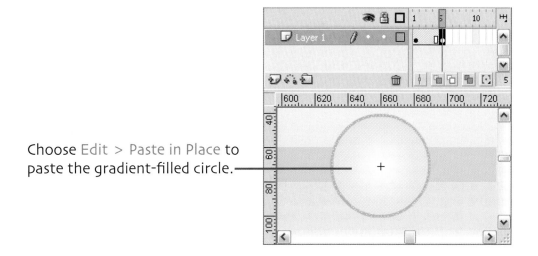

Choose Edit > Paste in Place to paste the gradient-filled circle.

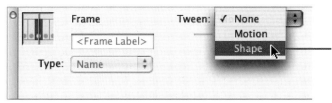

Select Frame 1. In the Property Inspector, set the Interpolate drop-down menu to Shape.

Press (←Enter) to preview the animation.

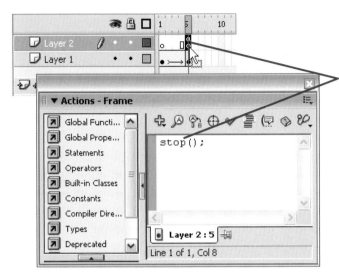

We need to add a Stop Action, or the animation will loop repeatedly when the user's mouse is over the button. Add a new layer. Insert a keyframe in Frame 5. Enter stop(); in the Actions panel.

Click btn_gallery in the Edit bar to exit symbol-editing mode for the movie clip.

For our Down state we want to move the objects down and to the right 1 pixel. Move the Playhead to the Down frame, and choose Edit > Select All to select the text and circle.

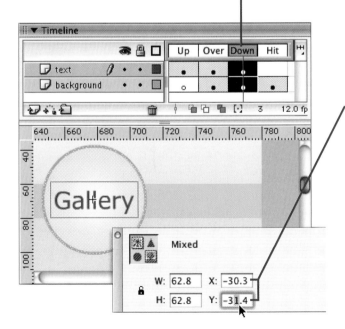

In the Property Inspector, add 1 to the x and y values of the selection. The values are negative, so if x = -31, change it to -30. Do the same for y.

We're done editing the button, so exit symbol-editing mode.

The Enable Simple Buttons feature won't show us the animated Over state, so we'll have to preview our buttons in the Flash Player. Choose Control > Test Movie, or press Control ←Enter (Windows) or ⌘ ←Enter (Mac).

add button sound

As the final touch to our button, we're going to add a click sound to the Down state.

Choose File > Import > Import to Library. In the Import to Library dialog, navigate to the development_files folder. Select the file btn_click.wav, and click Open.

Double-click the Gallery button to edit it. Add a new layer, and name it sound. Add a keyframe to the Down frame.

In the Library panel, click btn_click.wav, and drag it onto the Stage.

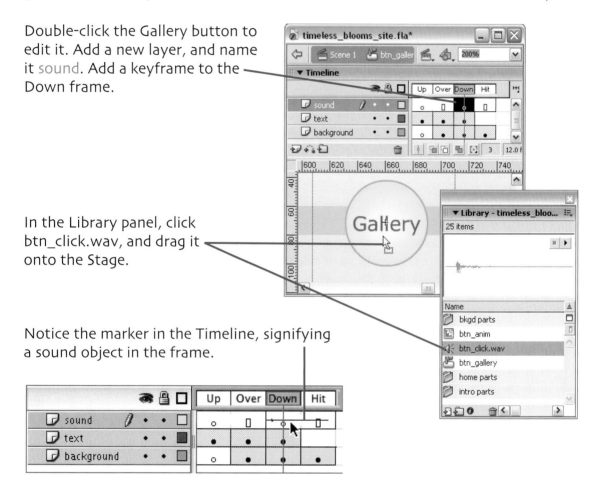

Notice the marker in the Timeline, signifying a sound object in the frame.

Exit symbol-editing mode.

If you want to test the sound, turn on Enable Simple Buttons.

duplicate buttons

Now that we've completed our button design, we need to make copies for each of the other sections of our site.

In the Library panel, right-click (Windows) or Control-click (Mac) the btn_gallery symbol, and choose Duplicate from the drop-down menu.

In the Duplicate Symbol dialog, name the symbol btn_home, and click OK.

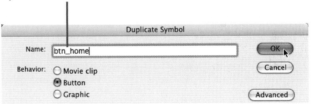

duplicate buttons (cont.)

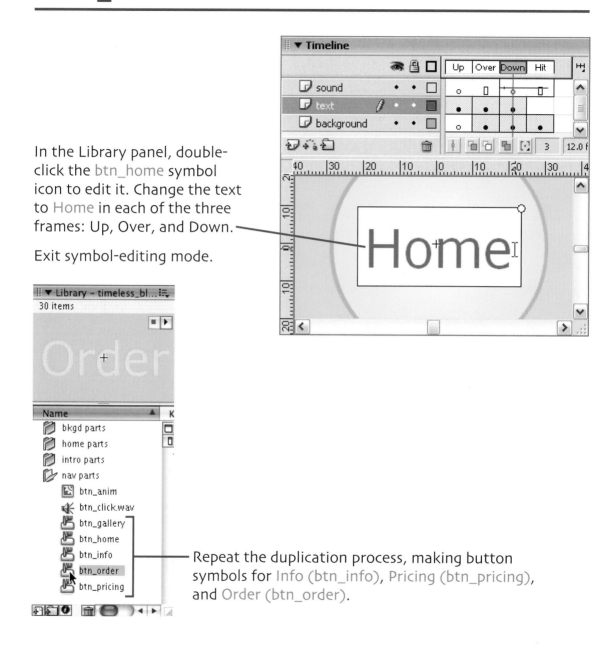

In the Library panel, double-click the btn_home symbol icon to edit it. Change the text to Home in each of the three frames: Up, Over, and Down.

Exit symbol-editing mode.

Repeat the duplication process, making button symbols for Info (btn_info), Pricing (btn_pricing), and Order (btn_order).

layout buttons

With a button for each of our sections complete, we can add them to the layout.

From the Library panel, drag out an instance of each of the buttons into the buttons layer, ordering them as shown here. (Don't worry about spacing or alignment; we'll fix that in a minute.)

With the Selection tool, click outside the Stage, and drag a selection marquee around the buttons to select them all.

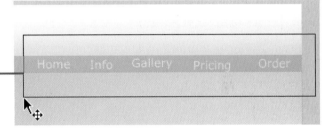

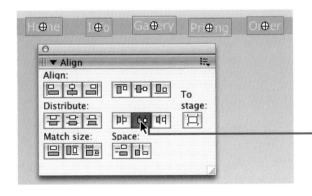

Choose Window > Design Panels > Align to open the Align panel. Click the Distribute Horizontal Center button to evenly space the buttons.

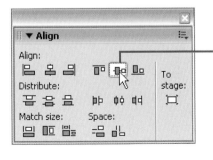

Click the Align Vertical Center button to align the buttons.

add sections to the site

Having buttons in our site is great, but we don't have anywhere for them to point to. We need to add the other sections of our site to the Timeline.

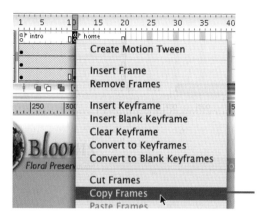

In the Timeline, select keyframe home in the actions layer.

Copy the frame.

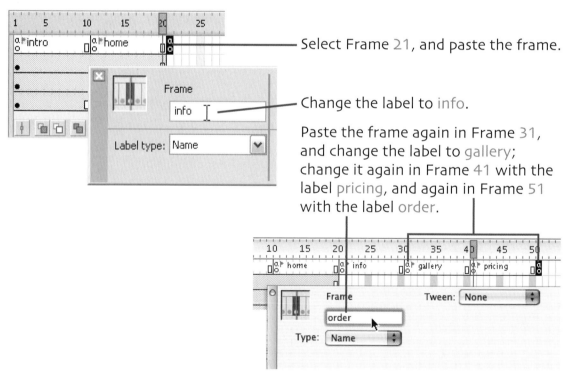

Select Frame 21, and paste the frame.

Change the label to info.

Paste the frame again in Frame 31, and change the label to gallery; change it again in Frame 41 with the label pricing, and again in Frame 51 with the label order.

Select Frame 60, and press F5 to insert frames.

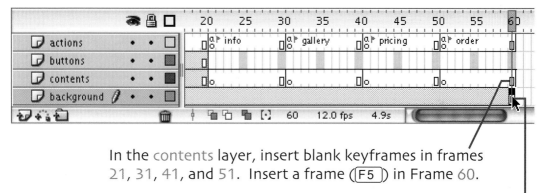

In the contents layer, insert blank keyframes in frames 21, 31, 41, and 51. Insert a frame (F5) in Frame 60.

In the background layer, insert a frame (F5) in Frame 60.

add actionscript

With our site sections defined, we have places for the buttons to navigate to. Let's add the navigation controls.

Move the Playhead back to Frame 1. Select the Home button.

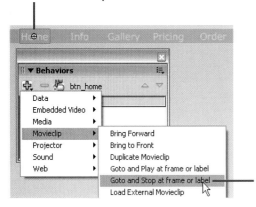

Open the Behaviors panel. Click the Add Behavior button. In the drop-down menu, choose Movieclip > Goto and Stop at frame or label.

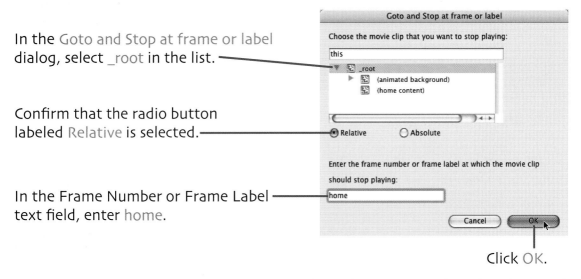

In the Goto and Stop at frame or label dialog, select _root in the list.

Confirm that the radio button labeled Relative is selected.

In the Frame Number or Frame Label text field, enter home.

Click OK.

The behavior is now listed in the panel and can be edited later, if necessary.

build a navigation system

Select the Info button. Repeat the steps to add the Goto and Stop at Frame or Label behavior. Enter info in the Frame Number or Frame Label text field.

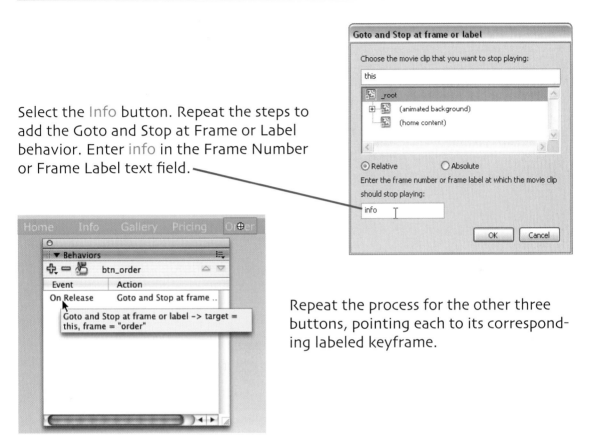

Repeat the process for the other three buttons, pointing each to its corresponding labeled keyframe.

With the behaviors attached, we're ready to copy the buttons to the other sections. In the buttons layer, insert keyframes in frames 21, 31, 41, and 51.

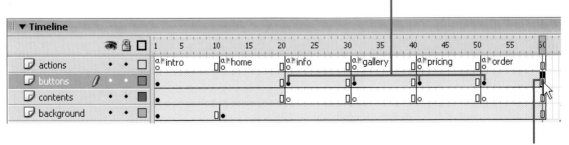

Add a frame (F5) in Frame 60.

alter button behavior

We want to provide viewers with a visual cue of where they are within the Web site. We do that by displaying the Down state of the corresponding button in each section of the site.

We can instruct Flash to treat a button symbol as a graphic, rather than as a button, to disable it and display its Down state.

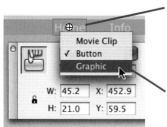

Move the Playhead to Frame 1, and select the Home button.

In the Property Inspector, click the Symbol Behavior drop-down menu, and choose Graphic.

A dialog appears warning that the ActionScript will be deleted from the button. Click OK.

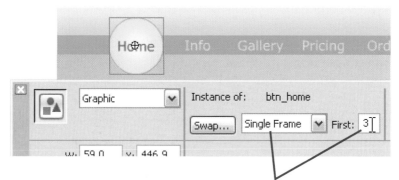

Click the Options for Graphics drop-down, and choose Single Frame. Enter 3 in the First Frame field. The third (Down) frame of the button symbol is displayed.

Move the Playhead to Frame 21, and select the Info button. In the Property Inspector, set the same attributes that you did for the Home button.

Step through the remaining three sections, repeating the process in each.

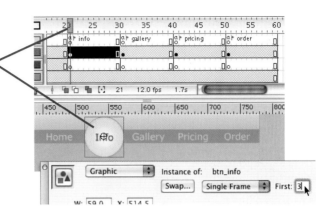

Press (Control)(←Enter) (Windows) or (⌘)(←Enter) (Mac) to preview your work and test your button navigation in the Flash Player window.

You've now successfully created a navigation system for your site!

Save your file.

extra bits

create buttons p. 80

- Button symbols provide an easy method for creating the type of interactive, multi-state button we're accustomed to seeing on the Web. Buttons have different images (referred to as states) that display based upon user action. The Up state displays by default; the Over state displays when the user moves the mouse over the button; and the Down state displays when the button is clicked. A fourth state, Hit, is never displayed but is used to define the active area of the button.

- In most cases, you'll use the same graphic elements for all of your buttons. When you're working out the design, work with the text of the longest name you'll need. This ensures that the graphic fits all of your buttons and you won't have to make frustrating fixes later. In our project, we start with the Gallery button because it is just a little bit wider than Pricing.

7. add inside sections of the web site

In this chapter, we work on developing the content for the different sections of our Web site. We'll accomplish the following:

Add a progress bar to update viewers when a large file is downloading.

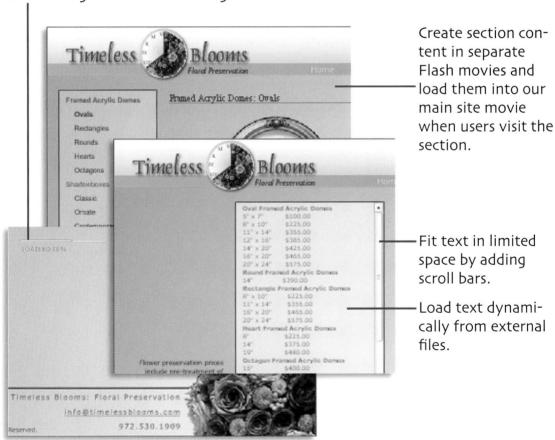

Create section content in separate Flash movies and load them into our main site movie when users visit the section.

Fit text in limited space by adding scroll bars.

Load text dynamically from external files.

build separate movies

If your Flash file takes too long to load when users visit the site, you run the risk of driving them away. One way we reduce that likelihood is by creating content for the site in separate Flash movies that are downloaded into our main movie when they're needed, as the user moves through the site.

For instance, when users go to the Gallery section of the site, they'll be viewing the Gallery keyframe of our main movie (timeless_blooms_site.swf) with another movie (contentGallery.swf) loaded into the frame.

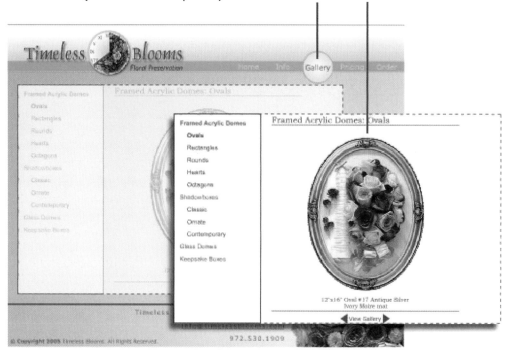

We'll learn the mechanics of loading movies a little later. First we need to create a movie to load.

add inside sections of the web site

create scrolling text

There is more text for the Info section than will fit within the content area of our layout. To fit the text into the area, we'll create a text box with an attached scroll bar component. (See extra bits on Page 120.)

Choose File > Open. In the Open dialog, locate the file contentInfo.fla that you downloaded from this book's companion site and copied into the site's development_files folder. Select the file, and click Open.

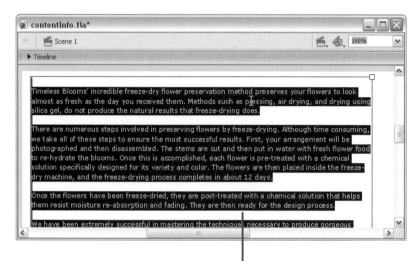

The file contains one large text box with all the copy for the Info section. Double-click the text box, and choose Edit > Select All. Choose Edit > Cut, or press Ctrl X (Windows) or ⌘ X (Mac) to move the text box to the clipboard. We'll paste the text into a special text box later.

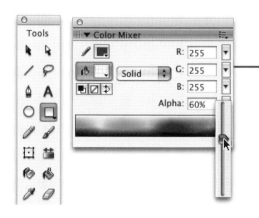

Select the Rectangle tool. In the Color Mixer panel (Window > Design Panels > Color Mixer), click the Stroke color well, and choose our dark rose color from the pop-up swatches pane. Click the Fill color well, and choose white. Change the Alpha value to 60%.

create scrolling text (cont.)

Click the top-left corner of the Stage, and drag out a 640 X 395 pixel rectangle (this matches the dimensions of the usable area in our site design). Check the location and size values in the Property Inspector, and change them if you need to.

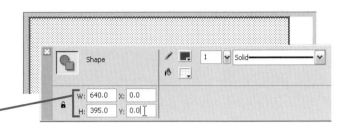

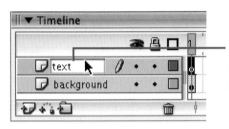

Add a new layer to the Timeline, and name it text. Click on the Stage to reset the Property Inspector.

Select the Text tool, and set the following attributes in the Property Inspector:

Text Type: Dynamic Text

Font: Verdana   Font Size: 11

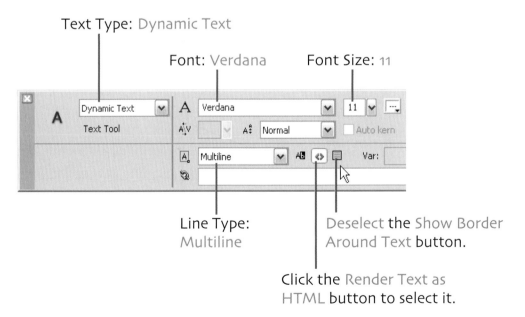

Line Type: Multiline

Deselect the Show Border Around Text button.

Click the Render Text as HTML button to select it.

Click the Stage near the top-left corner, and drag out a text box close to the size of the background rectangle.

Choose the Selection tool. Choose Text > Scrollable to make the box accept more text than will fit within its dimensions.

In the Property Inspector, change the Text box placement and size as shown.

Give the text box the Instance Name textInfo.

Double-click the text box to edit it. Paste the text you copied earlier into the text box (Edit > Paste). The text is inserted in the box, and the end of the text is displayed.

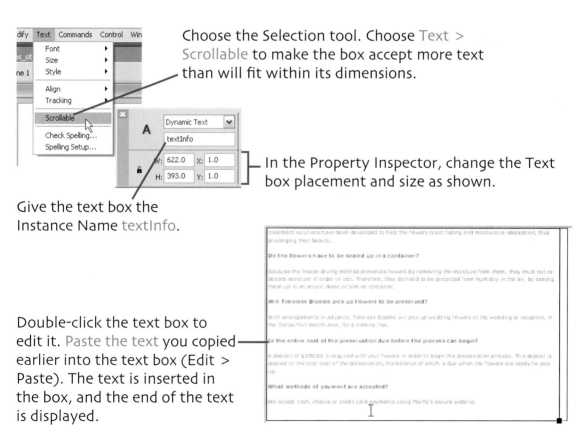

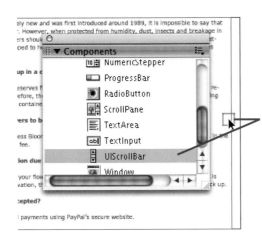

Choose Window > Development Panels > Components to open the Components panel. Click the UIScrollBar component, and drag it onto the Stage, just overlapping the right edge of the text box, and release. The component snaps to the right of the text box and automatically resizes its height to match the box's.

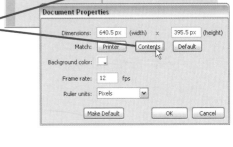

Finally, we need to shrink the Stage to fit our content. Click the Stage to deselect the UIScrollBar component. In the Property Inspector, click the Document Properties button. In the Document Properties dialog, click the Match Contents button to resize the Stage, and click OK.

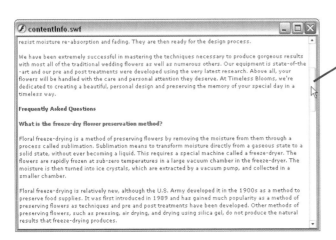

Test the movie, Control ←Enter (Windows) or ⌘ ←Enter (Mac), to view the working scrollbar. Close the Flash Player window.

When we test a movie, Flash exports a SWF movie file to play in the Flash Player, placing it in the same directory as the Flash file. Since we have no special publishing requirements for this movie, we can use that SWF to load into our main movie.

Save and close the Flash file contentInfo.fla.

load external movies

Back in our main Flash file (timeless_blooms_site.fla), we need to set up the file to load the contentInfo.swf movie into the Info section.

Move the Playhead to Frame 21. The text Capture the MEMORIES looks kind of funny out of the context of the home page content and is taking up valuable Stage area that we could use for content. Let's make another background without the text.

In the Library panel, right-click (Windows) or (Control)-click (Mac) the background symbol. Choose Duplicate from the drop-down menu. In the Duplicate Symbol dialog, name the symbol background_no_text, and click OK.

Double-click the background_no_text symbol icon in the Library panel to open it for editing.

Select the two text boxes containing the words Capture the Memories, and delete them. Click Scene 1 in the Edit bar to exit symbol-editing mode.

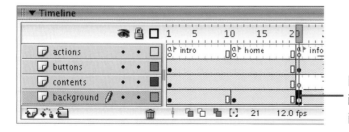

In the Timeline, select Frame 21 in the background layer, and insert a keyframe.

load external movies (cont.)

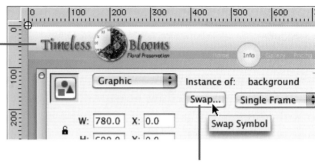

With the Selection tool, click to select the background symbol on the Stage.

In the Property Inspector, click the Swap button.

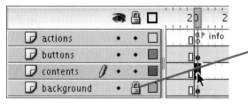

In the Swap Symbol dialog, select background_no_text, and click OK.

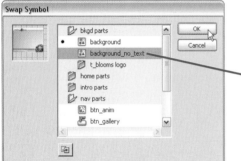

In the Layers column of the Timeline, click in the Lock column of the background layer to lock the layer so we don't accidentally select it as we work on content. Select Frame 21 in the contents layer.

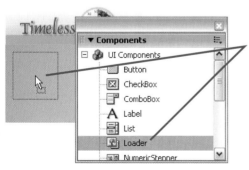

In the Components panel, click the Loader component, and drag it onto the Stage. A Loader Component symbol has been added to the Library, so we'll be able to reuse the symbol in other sections.

add inside sections of the web site

Use the Property Inspector to position the Loader symbol at x: 20 and y: 105. Name the symbol instance loaderInfo.

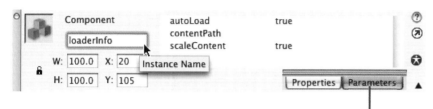

Component symbols have special properties, parameters that you can set to specify different behaviors. Some of the parameters are displayed in the Parameters tab that is now visible in the Property Inspector, but a more complete set of parameters are displayed in the Component Inspector panel.

Open the Component Inspector panel (Window > Development Panels > Component Inspector). Enter contentInfo.swf in the Value field for the contentPath parameter.

Click in the scaleContent parameter value field, and select false in the drop-down menu. This instructs Flash to display our movie at its actual size, not sizing it to the 100 X 100 dimensions of the Loader symbol.

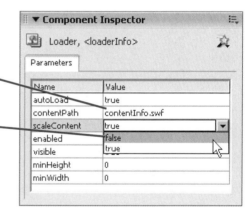

Choose Control > Test Movie, or press (Control)(←Enter) (Windows) or ⌘(←Enter) (Mac). When the movie appears in the Flash Player window, click the Info button.

You see that our contentInfo movie with its scrolling text box is displayed in the content area exactly as we wanted.

Close the Flash Player window.

add inside sections of the web site   **109**

load external text

If you have text content for your site that changes on occasion, like a price list, you can put the information in a text (TXT) file with simple HTML formatting and load it into your movie. This makes updating the content much faster and easier—you can update the text file independent of your Flash movie. (See extra bits on Page 120.)

We'll load a text file that contains the Timeless Blooms price list into a movie (contentPricing.swf) that will load into our main movie. First we'll set up the Loader while we're in our main file.

Select the Loader symbol instance that loads the Info content, and copy it to the clipboard. Select Frame 41 in the contents layer, and choose Edit > Paste in Place.

With the Loader symbol selected, change the Instance Name to loaderPricing in the Property Inspector. Change the contentPath value to content-Pricing.swf.

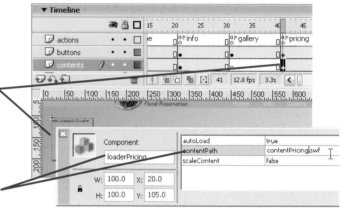

The Loader is ready; now we just have to create the movie. Open the file contentPricing.fla, located in the development_files folder.

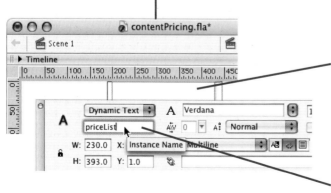

With the Selection tool, select the text box in the middle of the Stage.

In the Property Inspector, note that this text box is already set to Dynamic Text and that the Render Text as HTML button is selected. Change the Instance Name to priceList.

add inside sections of the web site

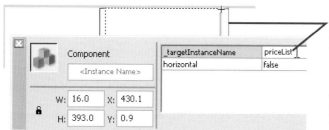

Select the UIScrollBar Component symbol that is attached to the right of the text box. In the Property Inspector, change the _targetInstanceName value to priceList to link the scroll bar to the text box.

Select Frame 1 in the actions layer. In the Actions panel, enter the code exactly as you see it here:

```
loadMyFile = new LoadVars()
loadMyFile.onLoad = function ()
{
    priceList.htmlText = this.priceList;
}
loadMyFile.load("contentPricing.txt");
```

Save the file, and minimize the Flash application to view your desktop.

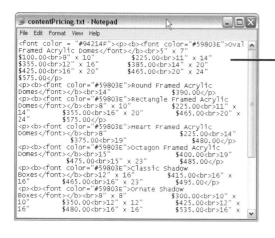

Locate your development_files folder. Inside the folder, locate the file contentPricing.txt. This is the text file containing our price list information. We need to open it and add some text that identifies it for Flash. Double-click to open the file. The file will open in Notepad (Windows) or TextEdit (Mac).

You'll note that the text file is not formatted in a standard way with carriage returns; this is required to have the text appear correctly when loaded into the dynamic text box in Flash.

load external text (cont.)

Click to place the insertion point at the beginning of the file, before the text < font.

Enter priceList =. Save and close the file.

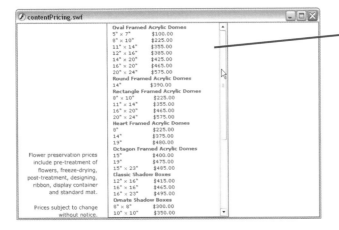

Make the Flash application visible again and test the movie, Control ←Enter (Windows) or ⌘ ←Enter (Mac). You'll see that the text box has been populated with the contents of the text file.

Close the Flash Player window. Save the Flash file content Pricing.fla, and close it.

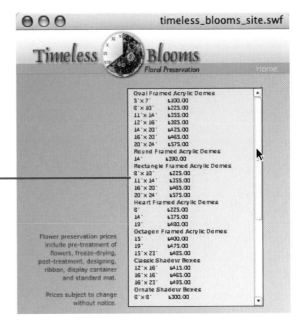

Back in the file timeless_blooms_site. fla, test your movie, Control ←Enter (Windows) or ⌘ ←Enter (Mac). When the movie appears in the Flash Player window, click the Pricing button to see your price list.

Close the Flash Player window.

add inside sections of the web site

link to external pages

We can link to and open external Web pages from within our Flash file. Those pages may be within our site or elsewhere on the Web. In this step, we'll add a link in the Order section movie that opens an HTML file containing an order form.

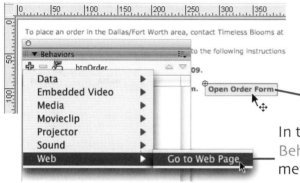

Open the file contentOrder.fla, located in the development_files folder.

With the Selection tool, select the Open Order Form button.

In the Behaviors panel, click the Add Behavior button. In the drop-down menu, choose Web > Go to Web Page.

In the Go to URL dialog, enter order_form. htm (included in the development_files folder) in the URL field. Choose "_blank" from the Open in drop-down menu to open the link in a new browser window.

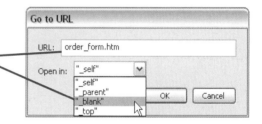

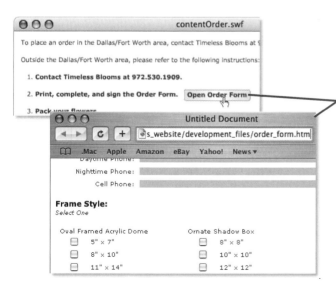

Test the movie, Control +Enter (Windows) or ⌘ +Enter (Mac). When the movie appears in the Flash Player window, click the Open Order Form button, and the HTML file should launch into a new browser window.

Close the browser window, and switch back to the Flash application. Close the Flash Player window.

Save and close contentOrder.fla.

add inside sections of the web site   **113**

link to external pages

Now we need to place a Loader in the Order section of our main movie to load the contentOrder.swf movie.

In the file timeless_blooms_site.fla, move the Playhead to Frame 41.

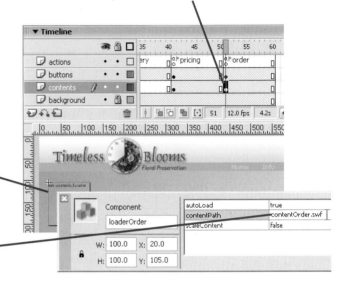

Select the Loader component instance, and copy it to the clipboard. Move the Playhead to Frame 51, and choose Edit > Paste in Place. Click the symbol to display its properties in the Property Inspector.

Change the Instance Name to loaderOrder. Change the contentPath value to contentOrder.swf.

Test the movie, Control +Enter (Windows) or ⌘ +Enter (Mac). When the movie appears in the Flash Player window, click the Order button. Click the Open Order Form button to see the HTML file launched into a new browser window.

Close the browser window, and switch back to the Flash application. Close the Flash Player window.

slide show controls

Finally, a Web site like ours would be incomplete without samples of the beautiful work.

In this step, we open an existing Flash file with images and standard button navigation. We'll add buttons that make it a slide show, moving the Playhead to the next or previous frames in the Timeline.

Open the file contentGallery.fla, located in the development_files folder. Move the Playhead between several frames and note how the file is set up with buttons on the left side.

Select the slide show layer. Open the Library panel for this file and drag out an instance of the btn_prev symbol. Place the symbol instance at the left of the text View Gallery.

In the Property Inspector, enter prev_btn in the Instance Name field.

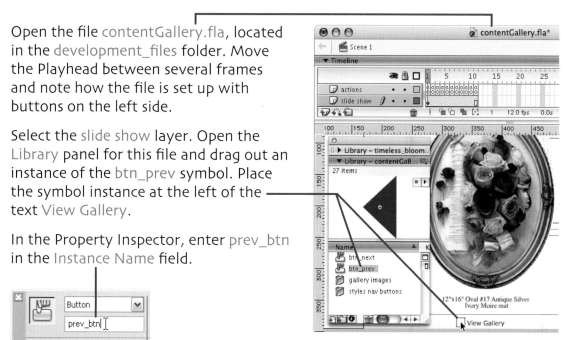

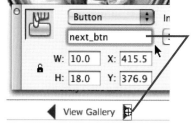

Drag an instance of the btn_next symbol to the right of the View Gallery text. Name the instance next_btn.

slide show controls (cont.)

Select Frame 1 of the actions layer. In the Actions panel, click after stop(); to place the insertion point, and press ←Enter twice.

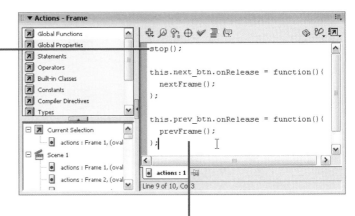

Enter the code shown here exactly as you see it:

```
this.next_btn.onRelease = function(){
    nextFrame();
};

this.prev_btn.onRelease = function(){
    prevFrame();
};
```

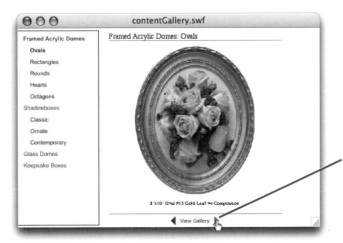

Note the text in the first line of each section that references the Instance Names you assigned to the button symbols.

You've just created slide show controls that you can reuse in your own projects. Test the movie, Control ←Enter (Windows) or ⌘ ←Enter (Mac), to see the buttons in action.

Close the Flash Player window.

add inside sections of the web site

add progress bar

As you might imagine, the number of images in the gallery movie dramatically increase the file size. When you're loading a large file, it's a good idea to provide some feedback for the user to let them know what's happening and how long they can expect it to take.

In this section we'll add a progress bar that appears while the gallery movie loads.

First, we need to set up the Loader for our gallery movie. In the timeless_blooms_site.fla file, select Frame 51 in the contents layer. Select the Loader component instance, and copy it to the clipboard.

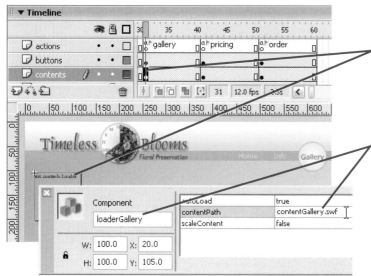

Move the Playhead to Frame 31, and choose Edit > Paste in Place. Click the symbol to display its properties in the Property Inspector. Change the Instance Name to loaderGallery. Change the contentPath value to contentGallery.swf.

In the Components panel, select the ProgressBar component. Drag the component into the center of the Stage.

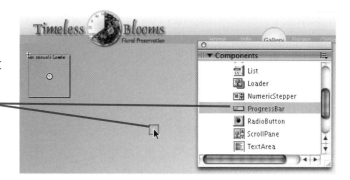

add progress bar (cont.)

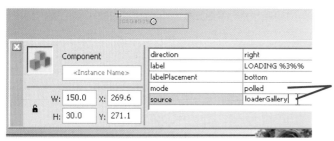

The component symbol is added to the Library, and the Parameters tab appears in the Property Inspector. Click the Mode parameter drop-down menu, and choose polled. Enter loaderGallery in the Source parameter field, pointing the progress bar to the loader it will monitor.

With the component still selected, enter this code in the Actions panel to tell the component to disappear when the download completes:

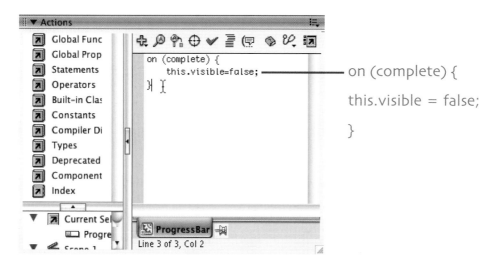

```
on (complete) {
    this.visible = false;
}
```

Test the movie, Control ←Enter (Windows) or ⌘ ←Enter (Mac). When the movie appears in the Flash Player window, click the Gallery button. Because the gallery file is loaded from your hard drive and not over the Internet, it may load too quickly for you to see the progress bar in action.

add inside sections of the web site

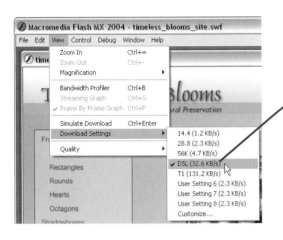

You can simulate a slower network connection with Flash's Simulate Download feature. With the Flash Player window still open, choose View > Download Settings > DSL (32.6 KB/s).

Choose View > Simulate Download, or press [Control][←Enter] (Windows) or [⌘][←Enter] (Mac).

When the main movie loads, press the Gallery button and watch your progress bar in action.

Close the Flash Player window.

All of our site sections are now filled with content. We're ready to prepare our files for upload to the Web.

Save your file.

extra bits

create scrolling text p. 103

- Dynamic text boxes, as the name implies, are designed to serve as containers for text from other sources (typically text loaded at run time). For that reason, you can't format individual text selections inside a dynamic text box. Any changes made via the Property Inspector are applied to all the text in the box. Additionally, dynamic text boxes have limited support for formatting applied to the source text.

  In our exercise, the text was formatted in a standard static text box using only rudimentary formatting options such as Bold and Font Color. If you were to select the static text box and change its setting to Dynamic, all formatting would disappear. To maintain our formatting, we copy or cut the text from the static (formattable) text box to the clipboard, and then paste it into the dynamic text box.

load external text p. 110

- Dynamic text boxes support a small subset of HTML formatting tags in loaded text. Only the following tags are supported:

  < a > anchor

  < a href = " " > hyperlink

  < b > bold

  < br > line break

  < font color > font color

  < font face > font

  < font size > font size

  < i > italic

  < img > image

  < li > list item

  < p > paragraph

  < u > underline

8. publish your web site

With development of all of our site sections complete, the only thing left to do is to ready our files for upload to the Web.

In this chapter we accomplish the following:

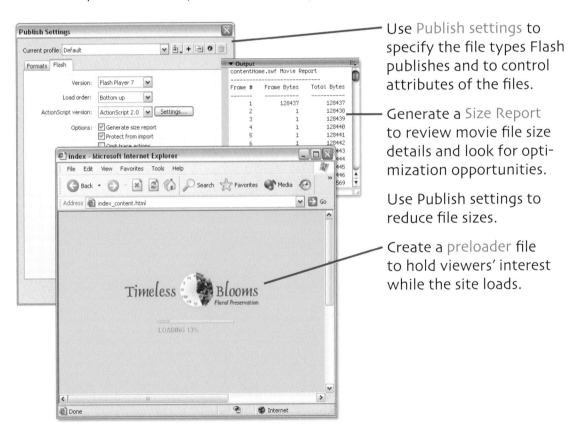

Use Publish settings to specify the file types Flash publishes and to control attributes of the files.

Generate a Size Report to review movie file size details and look for optimization opportunities.

Use Publish settings to reduce file sizes.

Create a preloader file to hold viewers' interest while the site loads.

swf settings

In Flash, we have the opportunity to specify different attributes for the files we're going to publish. In this section, we'll determine the Publish settings for our main site movie.

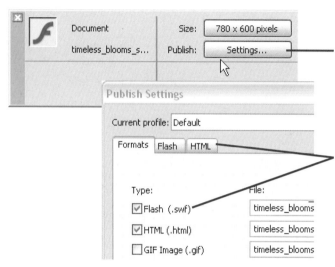

Choose File > Publish Settings, or click the Publish Settings button in the Property Inspector. The Publish Settings dialog appears.

In the Publish Settings dialog, there is one constant tab, Formats, and multiple other tabs that appear based upon the file types you choose in the Formats tab.

For now we only want to publish a SWF file. Choose the Formats tab, and click the checkbox next to HTML (.html) to deselect it. The HTML tab disappears.

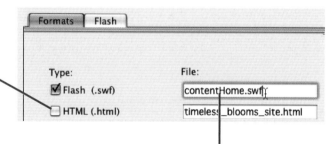

Note that Flash automatically assigns file names based on the name of the Flash file you're editing. Change the SWF Filename to contentHome.swf.

Click the Flash tab. The Version drop-down menu defaults to the Flash Player version associated with the version of Flash you're using. We won't change the setting.

Load Order determines in what order the Flash Player draws layers as the movie loads. Set the Load Order to Bottom up.

Leave the ActionScript version set to the default.

Click to select the Generate Size Report option.

Protect from Import prevents other people from importing your SWF file into Flash—protecting your work from theft. Click to select this option.

Ignore the Omit Trace Actions and Debugging Permitted options, as they are used for more advanced development than we've covered here.

Leave the Compress Movie option selected; it helps to reduce file size.

Leave the Password field blank; it's used in debugging.

Leave the JPEG Quality setting at 80.

Our one sound file was optimized before import, so we don't need to change anything in the Audio settings.

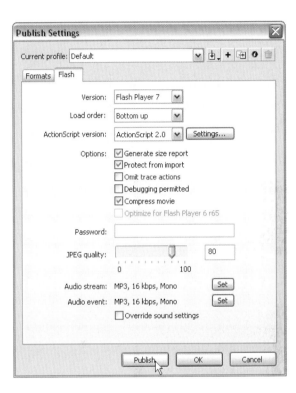

Click Publish. Click OK to close the Publish Settings dialog.

A new window, Output, appears. The window displays the Size Report, which has been generated for the SWF movie you've just published.

optimize file sizes

A Size Report provides a wealth of information about the size of your movie. In fact, the Size Report provides much more information than you need to understand. However, you can review the report to look for unusually large numbers that might lead you to think of ways to decrease file size.

The Total Byte column at Frame 60 (the final frame of the movie) shows that our movie is approximately 130,050 bytes or 130Kb—a bit large for someone on a slower connection. Let's see if we can find an optimization.

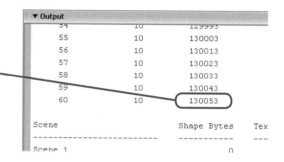

First, in the Frames detail, you'll see that large numbers of bytes are found in the keyframes 1, 11, 21, 31, 41, and 51. Note that these numbers do not represent the movies that we're loading in at run time.

Frame 1 provides the largest size hit because it includes our background components, intro animation, buttons, and all of the ActionScript classes needed to support the Actions throughout the movie.

The two next largest peaks in size are in frames 21 and 31 and can be explained by the addition of the Components we used there. We can't affect their size, so no optimizations are revealed.

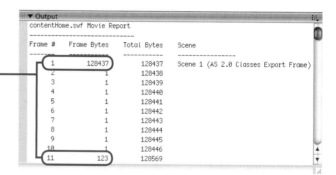

Scroll to the bottom of the document and look at the sizes of the four bitmaps included in our movie. Combined they add 34Kb to the total size. We can probably turn this discovery into an optimization opportunity.

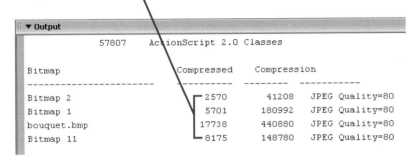

```
▼ Output
          57807      ActionScript 2.0 Classes

Bitmap                   Compressed    Compression
---------------------    ----------    -------- -----------
Bitmap 2                     2570          41208   JPEG Quality=80
Bitmap 1                     5701         180992   JPEG Quality=80
bouquet.bmp                 17738         440880   JPEG Quality=80
Bitmap 11                    8175         148780   JPEG Quality=80
```

Close the Output window.

Lowering the JPEG Quality setting in the Publish Settings dialog will lower file size. However it's important to remember that there is a trade-off of image quality. The best approach is to try different settings and see if you find the results acceptable.

First let's try a really low number, providing more file size savings but a much lower quality. Open the Publish Settings dialog, and change the JPEG Quality setting to 20.

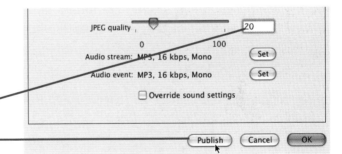

Click Publish. Click OK in the Publish Settings dialog.

```
▼ Output
       55           9          103818
       56           9          103827
       57           9          103836
       58           9          103845
       59           9          103854
       60           9          103863

Scene                      Shape Bytes
```

The Size Report shows that we've reduced the file size to just under 104Kb—a reduction of 26Kb. But what about the image quality?

Close the Output window.

publish your web site

optimize file sizes (cont.)

Test the movie, [Control][←Enter] (Windows) or [⌘][←Enter] (Mac). The quality of the images has degraded too much; we've set the quality too low. Close the Flash Player window.

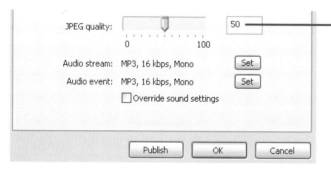

Click the Publish Settings button in the Property Inspector. Change the JPEG Quality setting to 50. Click OK.

Test the movie again. The Size Report shows a file size close to 114Kb (16Kb less than when we started), and the image quality is still good.

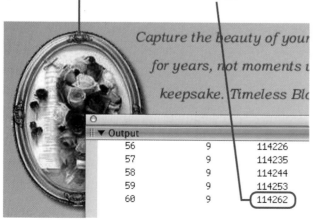

We'll go with these settings; however, we still have a pretty large file that could drive viewers away before it downloads. We'll work next to prevent that from happening.

create a preloader

Preloaders are the short animations and progress bars that play while a movie is loading. You've already created one preloader inside our site movie, the progress bar that plays while the gallery movie loads.

In this step, we create a fast-loading movie that contains only a logo, a Loader component that loads our main movie, and a ProgressBar component that provides download progress feedback to viewers.

When dealing with multiple movies loaded one into another, Flash Player can get confused by references to the Timeline—not understanding to which Timeline the reference points. We need to make one change in our main file to prevent this potential problem.

In the file timeless_blooms_site.fla, move the Playhead to Frame 31. Select the ProgressBar component.

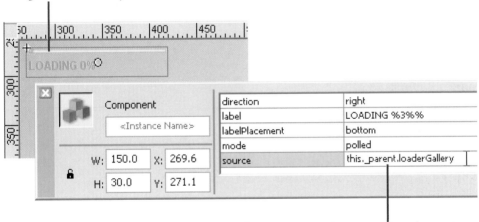

In the Property Inspector, change the source value to this._parent. loaderGallery. This new reference instructs Flash to look in this movie for the Loader component.

Choose File > Publish, or test the movie to generate an updated SWF file.

create a preloader (cont.)

Open the file index.fla, located in the development_files folder. The file has an animated logo symbol in the middle of the Stage.

Select Frame 1 in the loaded movie layer. From the Components panel, drag a Loader component to the top-left corner of the Stage.

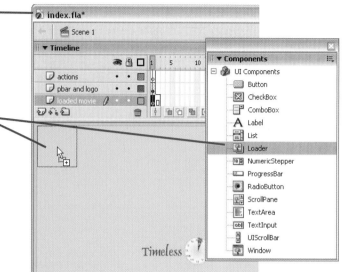

In the Property Inspector, make sure the component is placed at x: 0 and y: 0, and assign an Instance Name of loaderHome.

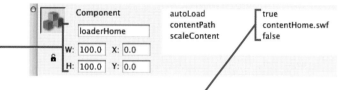

Enter contentHome.swf in the contentPath value field, and set the scaleContent drop-down menu to false.

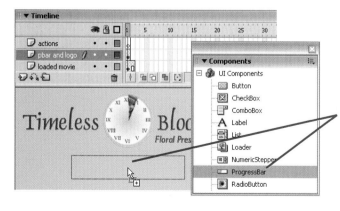

Select Frame 1 of the pbar and logo layer. From the Components panel, drag out a ProgressBar component, and center it just underneath the logo.

In the Property Inspector, assign an Instance Name of progressHome. Set the mode drop-down menu to polled, and enter this._parent.loaderHome for the source value to connect the Progress Bar with the Loader.

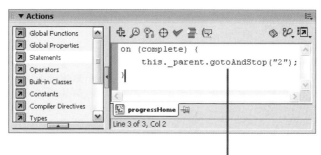

With the ProgressBar component still selected, enter this code in the Actions panel:

```
on (complete) {
    this._parent.gotoAndStop("2");
}
```

This code instructs Flash to move the Playhead to Frame 2 when the movie is completely loaded. Note that Frame 2 includes only the loaded movie layer, so the progress bar and logo will disappear.

Finally, select Frame 1 in the actions layer, and enter a stop Action (stop();) in the Actions panel.

Test the movie to watch the preloader in action. Close the Flash Player window.

publish your web site

html settings

Flash movies on the Web need to be wrapped in HTML files that provide movie display instructions to the browser. The HTML files can also include code that checks for the presence of the correct Flash Player plug-in and redirects the viewer if it's not there.

Luckily for us, Flash can publish the HTML files we need so we don't have to do the HTML coding ourselves.

In the index.fla file, click the Publish Settings button in the Property Inspector. In the Publish Settings dialog, select the Formats tab. Click the checkbox next to HTML (.html) to select it. An HTML tab appears.

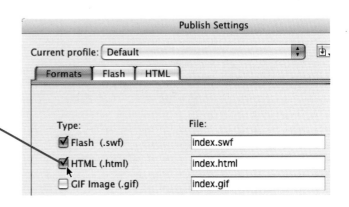

Select the HTML tab.

Flash generates the HTML file from a set of customizable templates designed for different Flash delivery requirements. Choose Flash Only from the Template drop-down menu.

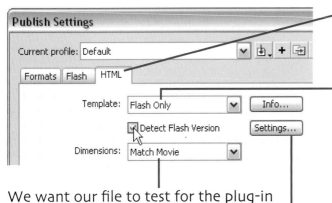

We want our file to test for the plug-in and to provide an alternate HTML file if the plug-in isn't present. Click the check box to select Detect Flash Version.

Click the Settings button.

publish your web site

In the Version Detection Settings dialog, note that Flash will generate three HTML files. The Detection File (index.html) will be our site's first file, the file to which other sites may link and the file that loads when our URL is entered in a browser.

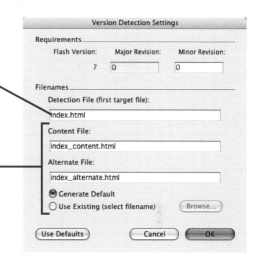

After the browser detection is executed, one of the other files will load—the Content file with our site movie or the Alternate file if the plug-in wasn't detected.

Click OK to close the Version Detection Settings dialog.

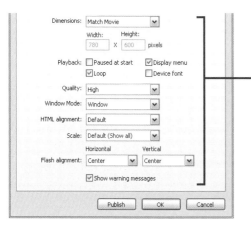

The remaining options in the HTML tab allow users to customize how their movies appear and behave in the browser window. For our purposes the default settings are appropriate, so we won't make any changes.

Select the Flash tab, and select Protect from Import.

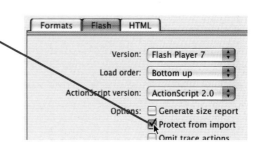

Click the Publish button to generate the SWF movie file and the HTML files we've requested. Click OK to close the dialog.

Save and close the files index.fla and timeless_blooms_site.fla. Choose File > Exit (Windows) or Flash > Quit Flash (Mac) to close the Flash application.

publish your web site

From your computer's Desktop, navigate to the development_files folder. You'll see that Flash has added the Flash movie (index.swf), the three HTML files (index.html, index_alternate. html, and index_content.html), one movie used in the Flash Player detection (flash_detection. swf) and one graphic file (alternate.gif) that is used in the alternate HTML file.

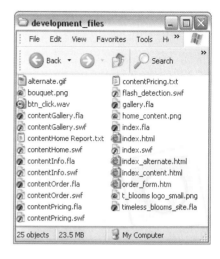

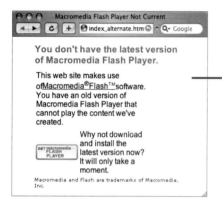

Before we see our movie working correctly in our HTML files, let's view the alternate file. Double-click index_alternate.html to open the file in the browser. This is what viewers will see if they don't have the correct Flash Player to view our site. You can customize this file using a text or HTML editor, if you want it to reflect the look of your site. Close the browser window and return to the development_files folder.

Double-click the file index.html to open it.

Because you have the correct plug-in (that was installed with the Flash application) you probably won't even be able to tell that the first file loads and executes browser detection before loading the index_content.html file.

collect files for upload

Our final step is to collect all of the files that will be uploaded to your Web server and copy them into the site_files folder.

The following is a list of the files to copy, along with brief descriptions:

alternate.gif—an image file used in the alternate HTML file

contentGallery.swf—Gallery section movie with samples slide show

contentHome.swf—our main site movie including the Home section, animated intro, and loaders for all the other sections

contentInfo.swf—Info section movie with scrolling text

contentOrder.swf—Order section movie with button that launches the order form into a separate browser window

contentPricing.swf—Pricing section movie with text loaded dynamically from a text file

contentPricing.txt—Text file with HTML formatting that loads into Pricing movie

flash_detection.swf—Movie embedded in index.html file and used for Flash Player detection

index.html—First file loaded when visiting our site; executes Flash Player detection and redirects based on results

index.swf—Preloader movie with progress bar and Loader

index_alternate.html—Page providing Flash Player download option when Player detection fails to find the correct plug-in

index_content.html—Page containing index.swf; our site is displayed in this page

order_form.htm—A Web page containing the Timeless Blooms Order Form; launched from the Order section

collect files for upload

Once you've copied all of these files into the site_files folder, you're ready to upload them using your FTP application and instructions from your Web hosting company or Internet service provider.

When you're done uploading, be sure to view your site via a browser and confirm that everything is working as it should.

That's it! You've successfully created and published a Web site using Flash. Now you have the know-how to create attractive, useful Flash-based Web sites all on your own. Enjoy!

index

index

Component Inspector, xviii, 109
components
    custom, xx
    defined, xviii
    Loader, 108–109, 110, 114, 117, 127–128
    ProgressBar, 117, 127, 128–129
    UIScrollBar, 106, 111
Components panel, xviii, 106, 108, 117
Compress Movie option, 123
containers, 30, 120
Content file, 131
contentGallery.fla, 115
contentGallery.swf, 102, 117, 133
contentHome.swf, 122, 128, 133
contentInfo.fla, 103, 106
contentInfo.swf, 106, 107, 109, 133
contentOrder.fla, 113
contentOrder.swf, 114, 133
contentPath parameter, 109
contentPricing.fla, 110
contentPricing.swf, 110, 133
contentPricing.txt, 111, 133
Convert to Keyframes command, 57
Convert to Symbol command, 19, 52, 56
Convert to Symbol dialog, 19, 52
Copy command, 36
Copy Frames command, 58, 94
copyright notices, 33
Create New Symbol dialog, 80
custom components, xx
Cut command, 23, 103
Cut Frames command, 67, 75

D

dashed lines, 36
Debugging Permitted option, 123
Delete Layer button, 74
Detect Flash Version option, 130
Detection File, 131
developer sites, 78

Development Files section, xii
Development Panels options, 106, 109
development_files folder, 2, 5
Distribute Horizontal Center button, 93
Document Properties button, 4, 106
Document Properties dialog, 4
Down state, 90, 98, 100
Duplicate command, 91, 107
Duplicate Symbol dialog, 91
dynamic text boxes, 110, 120

E

e-mail links, 31, 36
Edit bar, xiv, 32
editing handles, 15, 17–18
Effect Duration value, 74
Enable Simple Buttons feature, 86, 89, 90
Exchange, Macromedia, xx
Expand dialog, 59, 60, 62
Expand effect, 59
Expand Style options, 59
expanding text boxes, 31, 32
extra bits sections, xi

F

fade-in effect, 51, 52–53, 73
files. See also specific files
    collecting, 133
    creating, 3
    downloading, xii
    optimizing, 124–126
    saving, 5
    types of, 3
    uploading, 134
Fill color well, 11, 13
Fill Style drop-down menu, 13, 16
Fill Transform tool, 15, 17
film metaphor, xiii
Fireworks, 24, 30
Fireworks Objects folder, 25

Fireworks PNG Import Settings dialog, 24, 41
fixed-width text boxes, 31, 34
FLA files, 3. See also specific files
Flash
    and film metaphor, xiii
    interface, xiii–xviii
    intros, 55, 77–78
    more advanced books on, xix
    movies (See Flash movies)
    previewing animation in, 54
    scripting language (See ActionScript)
    terms, xiii
Flash-based applications, 50
Flash movies. See also animation
    adding ActionScript to, xvii
    building separate, 102
    controlling object stacking order in, 22
    controlling Playhead in, 47–48
    defining folder structure for, 2
    displaying information about, 124–125
    download considerations, xx, 102
    dressing the set for, 9
    file-size considerations, xx, 117, 124–126
    and film metaphor, xiii
    importing vector art into, 24
    linking to external pages from, 113–114
    loading external, 107–109
    multiple timelines for, 49, 50
    optimizing, 124–126
    previewing, 70
    providing display instructions for, 130
    testing, 106, 109
Flash Only option, 130
Flash Player
    detecting presence of, 130, 132, 133
    and movie testing, 106, 109
    and multiple movies, 127
    and Publish Settings dialog, 123

index

index

index

index